Praise for *New Ea*[...]

"*New Earth Journeys* is an on-the-edge-of-your-seat page turner! I was absolutely mesmerized.

An A-Z encyclopedia for understanding the most relevant issues regarding life in 2021 and beyond, complete with a how-to-navigate section for each topic.

This work is truly a guide for living. I will reference it often for its gifts of life-enhancing inner world practices, as well as its tips and strategies for interacting with the outer world.

Caroline Ryan and the Collective are blessing this world with stellar content, and I am so very grateful! Bravo!"

> - Kimberly Trefz, Creator & Host of The Happiness Retreat, whisper-words-of-wisdom.com

"*New Earth Journeys* is a beacon of light and a ray of hope for all of us, as we walk through what seem to be very dark days.

The Collective offers insights and practical information that are applicable for all of us in one way or another.

It is a book to be read cover to cover, savored, and returned to again and again."

> - Sally Schramp, Light Bringer

"*New Earth Journeys* is an essential guide for all Lightworkers, Ascension Guides, Starseeds, Wayshowers, and those newly awakened to the great shift.

The Collective comes through the author with brilliant clarity and resolve. A must-read for the next level of your work!"

> - Sherri Bausch, Ascension Guide and Light Language Coach, www.SherriBausch.com

"I strongly recommend *New Earth Journeys*.

"It is an energetically uplifting 'reference book' to help the ascending reader to navigate these challenging times of change, high discernment, and transformation.

The depth and clarity of the Collective's transmissions are a brilliant golden compendium of inner work guidance, knowledge, wisdom, and truth that supports the upleveling of consciousness to birth the New Earth human towards peace, freedom, and Unity consciousness."

    - Sonja Herman, Energy Healer,
      www.SonjaHerman.com

"When the race is almost done, when we are tempted to give in to absolute weariness, despair, and even anger . . .

The Collective, our head cheerleaders, push us on with their latest book, *New Earth Journeys*.

Every issue sent in by readers is about some crazy-making aspect of our current lives. Then come the calm, sound suggestions, followed by the blessed larger perspectives, and we recover and continue . . .

The chapters function as a kaleidoscope which reflects all the aspects of these 'Times of Crisis,' pivoting from personal focus to broader discussions of upcoming events on Earth and in the Galaxy, and the marvel of the role we all play throughout it all.

A really good read! Sprinkles of fairy dust throughout . . . small bits of humor sneak in here and there.

It's a book to return to after every rant! It will smooth our ruffled feathers!

And eventually, we'll 'get it'! And that is when we've really won!"

    - Penny C. C., Lightworker and Researcher

"*New Earth Journeys* is a must-read, particularly in this time of great change.

This marvelous book has helped me remember that I am not alone in my journey on Earth, nor was I ever!

Page by page, we receive continuous insights which give a profound understanding of who we really are. We get important reminders that we must remove the veil that has kept humanity shrouded in 3D consciousness.

That level of consciousness has kept us trapped in ignorance and fear, preventing us from claiming our own power.

As Caroline's guides remind us, the fifth dimension is ready to be entered. We only need to let go and let God.

Thank You, Caroline!"

>   - John R Fyfe, Vedic Astrologer/Palmist,
>   Healer and Author, www.therealjohnrfyfe.com

"The brilliant wisdom of these high-vibrational transmissions invites readers to remember and know their power, potential and role here on planet Earth, especially at this time.

The profound distinctions offered again and again invite the reader to slow down and embody these frequencies in order to usher in a life of peace and love."

>   - Diana (formerly Kelly S. Jones), The Wayshower -
>   www.SacredBeginnings.com

New Earth Journeys

The Collective Speak on Dealing with Personal and Global Crises

Caroline Oceana Ryan

Ascension Times Publishing

Text copyright © 2021 Caroline Oceana Ryan

Published by Ascension Times Publishing

ISBN: 9798786037921

New Earth Journeys: The Collective Speak on Dealing with Personal and Global Issues in Times of Crisis

Copyright © 2021 by Caroline Oceana Ryan

Book Four in The Fifth Dimensional Life Series

Cover design by Jen McCleary

All rights reserved. No part of this book may be used or reproduced in any manner whatsoever without written permission from the publisher, except in the case of brief quotations embodied in critical articles and reviews.

For more information, write to: ascensiontimes@gmail.com.

www.AscensionTimes.com

Published in the United States of America

DISCLAIMER: The information in this book, and all information written or channeled by Caroline Oceana Ryan in any manner or form, is not intended or implied to be a substitute for professional health or medical advice, diagnosis or treatment. Life results vary with each individual, and no results are guaranteed. No writing or channeling from Caroline Oceana Ryan or the Collective is meant or intended to diagnose, treat, cure, or prevent any disease or other life condition.

Dedication

*To our Spirit teams of Angelic guardians,
spirit guides, and higher self*

*To all of the Angelic legions and Archangels constantly
answering our calls for help and encouragement*

*To those who paved the way to Ascendancy—the Ascended
Masters, who by gaining enlightenment and developing their
Lightbodies, encouraged all of us to one day do the same*

*To the Star Nations, so powerfully present on and all around
the Earth now, assisting us in realizing our true selves and
our true power*

*And to every Lightworker walking the Red Road
to experiencing the higher dimensions while still in a
human body . . .*

*My profound thanks, Love, and respect for all you are and all
you do, at every moment*

Acknowledgments

Grateful thanks to early readers and reviewers of this book for their invaluable insights and support, and to my gifted graphic designer Jen McCleary and gifted book designer Neomie Apostol.

Many thanks as well to all who are reading and supporting this Fifth Dimensional Life series, the Ascension Manual series, and *Lennon Speaks*, or working with the guided meditations, reading the weekly Messages to Lightworkers, and being an active part of the Abundance Group.

To all those joining together now to create the cooperatives, communities, experiences, and fifth dimensional consciousness of the New Earth: I offer my Love and unending Appreciation.

As always, I honor and support your path of Light.

Table of Contents

Introduction i
1   On Feeling Numb During Times of Crisis and Accelerated Inner Growth 1
2   On Moving from Fear to Love 10
3   On Finally Hearing the Truth from the Mainstream Media 18
4   On Viruses, Jabs, and Coming Into Your Power 24
5   On Staying in Love, Joy, and Wonder 33
6   On the Power of Your Presence 41
7   On the Enactment of NESARA Law 47
8   On Resistance, and Stepping Up in a Time of Crisis 53
9   On Collective Consciousness and Assisting Others on Their Path 61
10 On Galactic Assistance with Healing and Restoring Lady Gaia 68
11 On Raising Children in Tumultuous Times 73
12 On the Jab and Being at Peace Amongst Divided Views 79
13 On Getting Along with Those Who Choose Differently from You 86
14 On Regaining Higher Dimensional Sight and Awareness 93
15 On Respecting Another's Path and Staying Calm Around Their Energies 99
About the Author 105
Other Books Channeled from the Collective 107

Introduction

This fourth book in the Collective's Fifth Dimensional Life series speaks to our current journey as we release thousands of years of third dimensional life, and lay the path for the New Earth.

Addressing issues in ways that help us keep our vibration high in the midst of crisis, the Collective speak on the power of the transformative higher Light flowing onto our planet now, and the Peace and fulfillment of reclaiming our Creator power. And so the word "crisis" is used here as being synonymous with new birth, and new forms of living.

Though no one can draw us a complete map to dealing with all the shifting challenges we see around us now, as with all of the Collective's books, these pages offer much higher wisdom, Love, compassion, and Light consciousness, while speaking directly to what we are experiencing now. The Collective offer their presence to assist us in celebrating our Ascension journey, and to remind us that we are never alone, even as we walk through the darkest night.

Be open to the wisdom offered here, which will often come as a download of energy that does not translate immediately into words. Yet in beautiful moments, we will find that it has flowed into our experience of life.

The questions you will find here are not my own, though I relate to many of them. As with all of the Collective's books, each chapter begins with a question from a Light Bringer, sent in from around the globe, by persons from all walks of life.

Their questions are being asked by millions of us now. The answers are offered with energies to lift both questioner and reader out of the quagmire of feeling defeated, alone, confused, or discouraged.

I ask that in taking in the insights from these channelings, you accept total responsibility for your own well-being—your own physical and emotional health, spiritual path, and outlook. Though the Collective do offer their insights on current medical crises and situations, neither they nor I claim to be a medical practitioner of any kind.

Please consider their work to be just one Light upon your path, not as a definitive "gospel" that must be adhered to, or a one-size-fits-all solution.

On all levels, your path is sacred and highly individual to you, and they and I fully respect such. Respect for all paths and choices at this time was one of the reasons this book came into being. So please take only what resonates intuitively as being right for your path at this time, and leave the rest.

Thank you for your powerful Light-filled presence during these early days of the New Earth and New Human! We are fulfilling the vision we held collectively before incarnating at this amazing time: Birthing fifth dimensional life into being an everyday reality on our planet.

We see the power of that Light breaking through in so many beautiful ways now. As the Collective like to say, "Great change is afoot!"

May their words and energies add more higher Light, Love, Wisdom, and Joy to your path.

Namaste, friend!

1

On Feeling Numb During Times of Crisis and Accelerated Inner Growth

Lately I have experienced an onslaught of inner growth and realization, which is probably a good thing, yet tiring. It leaves you feeling a bit overstretched at times.

In addition to that, we now hear of plans to restrict the public movements of those of us who will not take "the jab," alongside news of violence and unrest in countries such as Afghanistan, a failing economy, and personal issues such as the loss of loved ones.

Suddenly everything is being rewritten, and the old forms of calming and centering ourselves don't seem to be enough anymore.

I give up. How do we do this? I need to stay on keel, not only for the workday, but for my relationships, and my own well-being. And it's not pleasant, all this happening at once. I zone out and detach emotionally, and find it hard to meditate or even just talk to my guides and higher self, even when I really need to.

We are glad you have asked this! How to continue to progress in one's personal growth while handling what is happening in the world is one of the bigger issues of the day. We will speak of outer Earth issues throughout this book, but let us look first at what is happening to humanity.

Relatively few people on the planet have a conscious understanding of what is taking place in their own cellular structure, or in their own heart-mind now. This is so, though the current forms of Transformation are the most miraculous thing that could happen to humanity.

One of the things you are releasing in this moment of unyielding shift and change, is the instinct to use mainly your mind—your left-brain rational thought—to funnel understanding of a situation to the rest of your being. This involves not only your mental survival instincts, which are already highly alerted and exhausting most of you, including disturbing your sleep. It also includes the physical and emotional survival instincts that say, "This is too much newness at once! Get me off this boat—it might be sinking!"

Yet the human construct is not sinking. It is transforming.

The old construct, based on a two-strand DNA and fight-for-survival instinct, *was* sinking. But humanity's ongoing integration of the higher Light flowing onto your planet now, and your own decision to Ascend, has put you in a whole new vessel.

The ways that vessel operates are strange and new to you, and will not make sense many days. Yet they are far superior to the form humanity has been in for thousands of years. By the time the New Earth is in full bloom, old and New will not even be comparable.

You have heard of highly advanced technologies which are part organic and therefore sentient, and that work in symbiotic connection with the one directing them.

Now, this is an interesting issue, for several reasons. You live in an era in which nanoparticles are a part of your everyday life. They have been placed in your food, air, and water, as well as medical treatments, or what are touted as medical treatments. As many of you know, those metal fragments are not there to improve your quality of life.

On Feeling Numb During Times of Crisis and Accelerated Inner Growth

The nanoparticles are part of a plan to control and manipulate humanity on a more complete level. So that increasingly, more and more of your inner thoughts and outer life would be spurred on not by your true inner self, but by the direction transmitted to the "operating system" in your cells, which you would then respond to as any computerized system would.

We will not go into great detail regarding this agenda, as it is a dark one. And it is failing, despite much careful preparation. For one, the nanoparticles are being energetically deactivated, in part by your higher selves and souls, and in part by the cleansing and healing Light particles pouring in from your Sun. And by your galactic families, whose technology far exceeds that of the old Earth power structure, both in intricacy and in strength.

The low-vibrational transmissions do not so easily affect the New Human, such as you are all becoming.

Does that make the situation less dangerous and precarious? In many ways, yes, yet it will not feel to be so, some days.

This is because Earth's and humanity's emotional atmosphere has been calibrated to fear and panic. So that even if someone follows the latest channelings, meditates regularly, speaks with their Spirit team regularly, seeks a Divinely guided path, and so on, they can still feel threatened or isolated at times.

This is part of what you are experiencing when you say you feel numb and detached. Your survival instinct pushes you to detach from a situation that feels overwhelming to your logical mind.

This was a large part of the reason for isolating people from one another in the many "lockdown" scenarios over the last few years. When in isolation, people tend to panic far more, as their usual social/emotional supports and activities, which stabilize human emotion to a good degree, are suddenly not there.

During that time, the dial was pushed up as far as possible on the human emotional spectrum, via energetic transmissions and media manipulations intended to put people into a deep-seated panic. A supposed solution to the prevailing illness was then presented as a kind of savior to rescue humanity from perceived danger. And millions have gratefully leapt for it, without asking questions or using inner discernment.

Yet much of what the old power structure has been working hard to enact addresses the old human construct. More and more now, those plans do not apply to the increasingly fifth dimensional beings that millions of people are becoming. The low-vibrational transmissions put out to discourage Ascension (or any positive vibration) mainly address the old Earth systems. They do not so easily affect the New Human, such as you are all becoming.

Nor can they block the positive effects of the higher Light flowing to Earth. Or the effects of the many galactic and Angelic interventions and dispensations reaching you now. All very real, and very powerful.

And so the technology of the old ruling structure is based on a human construct that is increasingly defunct. Their entire global intent is out of place now, and falling off the current timeline.

Likewise, much of your left-brain reasoning, as it views your life and current Earth challenges, no longer applies. In its place is the increasingly higher intelligence of your cellular structure, your more integrated left- and right-brain thought processes, and your increasingly evolved spirit.

So that similar to the advanced technologies that are energetically (and benevolently) in touch with a user's inner intuitive commands, your body and spirit-mind are taking on a whole new way of sorting through the complexities of life.

You speak with others via energy transmission while visiting the higher dimensions, and as you travel etherically via space-time portals.

You will increasingly have less use for purely left-brain language, for one. Though words and their limited expressions will still have a place in human life, the spirit-mind is reaching beyond them into symbolic and even Angelic language, which is purely energetic in nature. You have heard people speaking in Light language. This will become more common, particularly among children.

Your lives are now increasingly intuitive in nature. This will not be surprising, for most of you. You use much intuitive higher technology in your sleep state when you travel in spirit form to Inner Earth, and when you are on the ships. In the sleep state, and as your higher self, you also speak with others via energy transmissions while in the higher dimensions, and as you travel etherically via space-time portals.

Though this form of living is far closer to your true nature than how you have lived in the third dimension, this shift will feel demanding and strange some days. Particularly as you attune to the leanings and understandings of your higher self, and ask that they move more fully into your Earth energies. The left-brain will not be able to keep up with nor know how to respect intuitive, heart-based reasoning. That is not reasoning in the sense that the mind requires, as that information often comes in without physical evidence to support it.

Not only do you feel to be speaking a different kind of language to your own planet now, you are also speaking in a whole different way to yourselves, and to one another. You are also taking in and relating to your outer reality in this new way.

And so your question is, given all that, how to stay on keel, for yourself and others? This question dovetails with all we shall speak on in this book. So let us look at how this parallels with what is happening to humanity.

We spoke of the nanoparticles, and the intent of the old power structure to use these to invade the human system, to inject a kind of operating system into the human bloodstream. This system then connects to a sort of mainframe computer that seeks to influence thoughts, words, actions, beliefs, rationales—the scope of a person's daily life.

Under those conditions, you would no longer be purely human, and could easily be denied the rights of being one. You would not even have the will to fight for those rights, unless you were permitted that by your controllers, and they would be unlikely to grant you that. Their desire has been to eradicate or enslave all nonwhite persons, and to erase from the planet those Caucasians whom they do not deem to be fitting servants.

So that when you say, "Suddenly everything is being rewritten, and the old forms of calming and centering ourselves don't seem to be enough anymore," you are speaking to more than you could know.

We do not wish for this or any of our writings to discourage anyone. Yet it is necessary to give some background on what is happening at present. And on how humanity has been manipulated to accept the current agenda, just as it has been manipulated to accept every other agenda, such as war, famine, separate social classes, income inequality, depression and anxiety, illness, toxins, and so on.

We do not tell people what to do in terms of their own life decisions. Yet we see that relatively few people have investigated fully the content of a particular "treatment" they are being convinced is necessary for their and their loved ones' survival. This is a mainly transparent scheme: You will note that the media's warnings and persuasions do not involve the terms "health and well-being" so much as "safety." Meaning, "threat to your survival."

Yet let us return to the issue of the intuitively guided ships and similar technologies. All of you have extensive knowledge of these in your higher aspects. Your higher mind is fully engaged during your sleep state, as you travel the galaxies and dimensions. It understands very well how to navigate the streams of energy that make life sensible. And how to maximize the beauty of energy flows and interchanges.

What you are producing now is near-instantaneous Creation, out of the magnificent sea of energy you live in.

In that higher vibrational state, there is very little conflict of views, unless one seeks out that kind of experience intentionally. Calm, centered living is consistently there for those who project that vibration.

Perhaps some of you are thinking, "If all is well with the higher vibrational beings, then why don't they come here, where people need help, and extend that to us! That's what I would do, were I living in some paradise without struggle or fears for survival. Without fear of losing what few freedoms are left to us!"

We would say, that is one of the greatest realizations you could come to at this point—to fully realize: You *did* come down to assist humanity!

You are amongst those many beautiful beings who came down to assist during the last days of third dimensional life! You decided to arrive in physical form to help via your vibration—to require that this planet be free once more—and you are doing that.

The fact that many of your soul family members are still in a higher vibrational state, without having incarnated upon the Earth in this era, does not mean that no one has arrived to assist, for you have many colleagues on this journey who stand with you in physical form.

We have been speaking of the intuitive connection the higher vibrational being has with their ship and other technologies—a hand on a console that appears blank, a look into a glassy screen, a thought directed to the technology—any of this can convey the user's wishes, and the technology responds as directed.

Your own mind/body/spirit is likewise evolving, so that you are more fully grasping the co-Creative nature of this Universe, including how that expresses in your immediate surroundings and outer life. And you are meant to do this without artificial intelligence being implanted into your being.

Beyond the Law of Attraction, what you are producing now is near-instantaneous Creation, out of the magnificent sea of raw energy you live in. You are capable of creating something new out of that ocean of energy, seemingly drawn out of the air.

Though you may feel and appear to be localized in one place and time, yet you are far greater than this, dear ones! You belong to the expanse of All That Is.

Your presence is itself the portal to this New Earth you seek.

Were you to go through your day wondering what next you might create—from projected thought, and feelings of Thankfulness and Appreciation, while ready to give at an equal level to what you desire to receive—this would transform your life, in very little time. You would need to be consistent and ongoing in the expectation that you are creating beautiful opportunities, relationships, and various forms of Abundance. A New Earth.

You are now at the point at which the ongoing potentials of the quantum field occur more clearly in everyday life and thought. And that changes everything. For you as individuals, and for all of humanity.

Understand that what you call "manifestation" does not fully describe the process we speak of. Because what you are taking on, as you move into co-Creation as a way of life, is an ongoing shift in your own vibrational field. A shift from feeling that you have little power over your own outer life, inner healing, and empowerment, into realizing you have endless power, though most of it is yet unclaimed.

You are both the Creator and the Creation.

The form of what you seek will not always come as you would prefer, if some other construct is preventing it. That too must be dealt with, and it involves healing those aspects of your spirit and psyche that carry very old pain and trauma. Yet it does not mean you do not have access to the very level of quantum mechanics that produces the outer result you desire. It simply means there is a journey between initial thought and creation that cannot be ignored.

And so this chapter serves mainly as an opening, not a definitive answer to this very great question, of how to remain inspired and positive while aware and empathic to the state of your planet and Her people.

For now, we would say, the desire to detach and close off, and not go deeper into any issue, even on a spiritual level, is understandable.

On Feeling Numb During Times of Crisis and Accelerated Inner Growth

Yet your human consciousness is the central power of energetic influence on the planet, and that will not cease. This was humanity's own decision. You came in for that very purpose. All else—the crystalline energy grid, the presence of Angels and Archangels, the elementals, ETs, Inner Earth Beings, and so on—pale in comparison to what you are achieving, *specifically because you are in human bodies at this time.*

You may feel that you are weaker for that, yet we assure you—your presence is the portal itself to this New Earth you seek.

More on that, as we go. For now, let us continue in this discussion, as we answer other questions . . .

2

On Moving from Fear to Love

How can we balance the duality/polarity within us, so that the outer world can also be balanced?
I feel as if I am on a giant pendulum, swinging wildly from Love to fear, with no relief in sight.

Your question addresses several areas at once. So we will speak first on why you are feeling these swings from one extreme to the other, then speak on how one can deal with the energetic surges running through your energy systems.

These surges relate to your physical and spiritual bodies, your mental outlook, your emotional balance. Your way of viewing the world. So that as you are in a state of Love for the world, or anyone, you are in a relaxed state of knowing that All Is Well. That whatever the outcome of life's circumstances, which are in constant, unpredictable flux now, you can relax. Relax in the inner Knowing that all is working out for the higher good of everyone on the planet.

On Moving from Fear to Love

Of course that is quite a statement to make, particularly now! You see so many leaving physical form now, to revert to their true form. That form is still a kind of body, but a far higher vibrational one than you have witnessed here on Earth for millennia.

You see the Earth Herself going through more shifts and changes than anyone could list, with both natural and manufactured disasters occurring. And you see bizarre and unexpected events happening in economies, in politics, in medicine—all areas of life.

And so you ask, *How do I stay out of fear, when my brain and body are hardwired for survival? They only know to panic when so much is unknown about everyday life. How do I stay calm in the midst of events that humanity has almost always been frightened of? It's all out of control!*

We want to look at that phrase "out of control" for a moment, because in actual fact, that is exactly what you came in to create.

Now, that will sound like complete nonsense—an idea that only adds to the dramatic swing from Love to fear. Yet it encapsulates perfectly what all Light Bearers are doing. You came to help dissolve the old forms of control over humanity, and these are the forms that have held human beings back from Ascending to higher vibrational levels for millennia.

What is interesting, is that during the 1950s and 1960s, many felt that life was going out of control then, too. Young people were identifying with forms of music that to older generations sounded cacophonous, even destructive at times. In fact, it was rock 'n roll that helped to vibrationally usher in an age in which the old power structure could no longer control human thought, feeling, and behavior anywhere near as fully as it had in the past.

Relax in the inner Knowing that all is working out for the higher good of everyone.

You will note that the old controllers then ushered in a drug abuse movement, designed to distract young people, engage them in destructive addictions, and hold them back vibrationally. Yet, again—the human desire to Ascend outran even those attempts. The healing qualities of hemp and cannabis were rediscovered, and a new awareness was born of the addictive nature of many things in human life, and the need to heal the wounds behind those compulsions. The spiritual journeys brought on by certain "psychedelic" substances also opened for many a form of release from the dark matrix mental programming.

Though we do not recommend the use of hallucinogens, we do understand those who take on expertly guided shamanic journeys of varying kinds, for the purpose of better understanding the nature and immensity of this Universe, as well as the nature and state of their own soul.

You came in to move things from a state of extreme control on the part of your former overlords, to a state of freedom for humanity. You are all part of the developing ability in human beings to release the construct and restrictions of the old Earth in favor of the freedoms, sovereignty, and self-realization of the New Earth.

This is a powerful breakthrough, particularly on a planet so long sunk into third dimensional ways! Never doubt that.

Of course you are concerned at times, as you see whole areas of life thrown into chaos and uncertainty. You are correct if you feel that is rooted in lower vibrations. Yet note that in Nature, nothing ever dissolves or breaks down and dies, but that something new can be birthed in its stead.

This is not "death" in the sense that you are taught. It is not a loss to be grieved. It is part of the birth process of that which you came in to birth, you who are midwives to the rebirth and Ascent of Earth consciousness.

You have, all of you, requested and required of all of us in the higher realms, including your soul families, to assist you in creating a fully renewed planet. One where the well-being of all is respected. One where notions such as living for profit, service to self, violence, exploitative power over living beings and Earth Herself are forever outlawed and dissolved, and superseded by the power and presence of Divine Love.

On Moving from Fear to Love

Move away from dense words and images, and affirm, "That is appearance, and appearance only. Divine Love is the only reality here."

And so we answered, by taking up the charge to support those who came to the Earth to establish a new realm here. A New Earth realm that would honor all life and create, via the establishing of NESARA law, a new and far higher level of existence, in accordance with Universal law, rather than in blatant violation of it.

Yet it is not by our action that life feels to be out of control, swinging wildly from Love to fear and back again. That is your action—your decision to break free from the now-defunct paradigm of a prison planet. You can mitigate your emotional extremes by deciding now that whenever your vibration dips down a bit, you will realize what is happening, and stop.

You will take a moment to consciously release panic or upset by breathing through these emotions. Allowing them, feeling them fully, thanking yourself for experiencing such, and breathing them out, full of self-compassion, without judgment.

In that moment of stillness, you are then able to move to a place of rest and quiet in which you do not demand answers or solutions. You are then able to allow your energies to move into a more neutral stance where you simply observe your thoughts and emotions, till you are able to flow your energies back up to the higher levels, reclaiming your power in that part of life.

You might also trace that downward spiral to the influence that reduced your vibration. You might be watching the news, for example—something we encourage you to do very little of now. So little of it is reliable information, and it is generally offered with a low and dense vibration. Difficult scenes and stories, accompanied by emotionally triggering terms and descriptions, can displace one emotionally.

Many of you have experienced similar situations in other lives to what you see happening on the Earth now, whether flood, fire, epidemic, or mass extermination. So to view any of these again is to retraumatize those parts of your heart-mind that remember quite well what it was like to experience those situations firsthand.

There are no accidents, no victims, no true losses.

Yet we would say, in that moment, bring up and release the old grief or shock. These are moments to realize what you have yet to heal, if you are able to feel your helplessness, grief, or anger without going into overwhelm. Allow those emotions to come up fully, then when ready, declare your Divinity—your I AM power. Then call all lost energies back into your being.

Regarding all dense words and images, declare: *"That is appearance, and appearance only. Divine Love is the only reality here."*

We wish we could tell you the power of that one thought, dear ones! It is unprecedented in scope and masterful in effect.

In that moment, you not only free yourself and millions of others from media manipulation intended to lower your vibration, and to keep you entrained to the sound of the newcasters' voices and their false, presumed authority. You also help free those who are being affected by that particular disaster, no matter how deeply embedded in it they may seem to be.

You may wonder, *How in the world could that be so? Those people are suffering, aren't they?*

And we would say, you help lift them out of suffering by sending them the empowering thought that they are so much bigger than any one thing that could ever happen to them—so much greater than any trauma they could suffer! And that they came in to experience what is occurring to them now. That there are no accidents, no victims, no true losses.

Even those who appear to lose their souls will somehow find their way home again, flowing as pure unmanifest energy back into the great stream of Light and intelligence that runs through All That Is.

On Moving from Fear to Love

That is what you have knocked out of "control"—that old system of manipulation which human beings have fallen prey to for millennia. You have helped knock humanity out of the old forms of humiliation, slavery, obedience to false authority, and steady belief (mental entrainment) in that which only pretends to be the Light.

As such, you and your fellow Light Bringers are to be congratulated. And yet, you do not want to lower your vibration each time your mind falls again into one of the old mental/emotional ruts you are still in the process of dissolving.

And so, in addition to protecting yourself from "False Evidence Appearing Real" (fear), we would say, replace the old habits of compulsive information-gathering, except for that which flows from Light-filled sources that carry healing energies. And release the old habit of desiring to connect with what you have known for a long time, simply because that feels safe and familiar.

Replace those pastimes with time in Nature, and time in meditation, or times of quiet. In speaking with your Spirit team. In engaging in whatever can be a form of meditation—playing an instrument, listening to high vibrational music, practicing yoga or Tai Chi, practicing some art or craft you can lose yourself in, playing with children, or spending time with animals. Giving to yourself and others in ways that make you Joyful. Flowing entirely into the present moment, while fully present in the body.

What we see amongst you Light Beings now, is the desire to move well beyond the "fight, flight or freeze" impulse.

Going into a state of fear is not so much a way to prevent things from happening as a defensive freeze of your energies. It is a way of hoping that your unsureness and anxiety will form a protective shell around you, to keep out the bad things you know of, and especially the bad things you do not know of, yet feel the possibility of.

Putting people into a state of fear is all that is required, generally, to control someone. Or at least, it was that way for a very long time. Your "reptilian brain," as they call it, often lives in a state of survival and vigilance, particularly if you experienced trauma in this or another life (as nearly everyone on the planet has).

Yet what we see amongst all of you Light Beings in human form now, is the desire to move well beyond the "fight, flight or freeze" impulse. So many of you have moved now into, "Why exactly should I react with fear, when we are in the quantum field? Things are so powerfully in flux on this planet, that none of these so-called impending disasters have to take place. Even that which *has* affected me or my community is not the last word on our well-being."

Do not scold or criticize yourself for those moments when you fall into stress or anxiety. There will be moments when you need to cry or beat a pillow in anger at what is happening in the world. This is not "unspiritual"! Allow those emotions to flow, as this is how you begin to heal them.

There will be other moments when you decide, "This is not me. This feeling is not mine," and move on. In those times, do something supportive for yourself, whether it's chanting an inspiring mantra, going for a brisk walk, turning on a sound healing recording, beating a drum, calling a friend, taking a shower . . .

Do not stress about duality as a concept or an apparent reality (in other words, a temporary appearance)—not in your life, or your planet's life. Release the need to notice polarities. Just move quietly and gracefully into a state that is calmer by being physically still and mentally quiet, even while you sit with your unsureness for a bit.

From there, move into a neutral state that may be neither Peaceful nor unhappy. And from there, up to hopeful, as you consider the potentials that lie in the quantum field, which awaits the orders of your expectations and images.

And from there—yes, on up the vibrational scale, back to Love again.

We encourage you to consider that Love is your natural state, even your default state of being. And to realize that no one controls your reality but you—you are the one who determines your responses to all you see and experience.

All that is real is within you, and that is entirely of your own creation, friends. Yes, even this time of apparent shift and tumult.

For this you came.

3

On Finally Hearing the Truth from the Mainstream Media

When will the truth be told to the misled brainwashed masses? When will the mainstream media (currently known as the lame-stream media) become uncontrolled, so that the truth may be told?

This is absolutely vital for any chance at moving forward and constructing a positive future. In my opinion, this has been held back for far too long. The longer people are kept in the dark, the harder the revelations will hit.

And have you heard any more from my buddy, Johnny Rhythm [John Lennon][1]? His words interweave with my question: "All I want is the truth / Just gimme some truth."

---

[1] This is a reference to the book channeled by Caroline Oceana Ryan, *Lennon Speaks: Messages from the Spirit of John Lennon* (2020).

On Finally Hearing the Truth from the Mainstream Media

They do indeed! And the energies embedded in those lines of music have been a Light on the path of many.

The one you knew as Lennon wishes now to say:

"Truth is coming down the line so fast and hard, it will feel like a freight train hitting the world when it finally happens in the fullest sense.

"On that day, everyone who has chosen to experience this New Earth reality will open their eyes, many for the first time, to understand who and what has been running the planet on their own terms, for their own shadowy purposes.

"Finally, there will be nowhere for that group to hide. Even now they are unable to hide from the Light, though they delude themselves daily that they are 'winning.' So many who once loyally served those beings have broken rank now, as they increasingly see that their false overlords are not winning. Not even close.

"You could almost feel sorry for those former overlords, yet they chose this dark path for their own reasons. They may follow it as they wish, but Earth is no longer their playground and their headquarters. She is hereby returned to Her own sovereignty, and to the stewardship of all who Love and honor Her.

"Yes! So much breaking through now. Don't even ask 'when'—say to yourselves every day, 'We are there! The Time is Now!'

"Of course, that's the only Time anyone ever has, and it turns out, that is enough."

* * * * *

Well said! And so we would also say, regarding when the mainstream media will be in a position to finally speak the truth, that there are many already amongst them who are assisting the Light Forces and the White Knights of the Ashtar Command in speaking the truth whenever possible.

Understand that mainstream media editors and managers have been warned to never allow their journalists to announce what many of them know to be true. Which is that each country and the planet as a whole has long lived under the tyrannical control you speak of. They are warned that they cannot speak of NESARA. Nor relay the underlying truth of what is really happening in any political or economic situation.

Situations such as covert weather manipulation and the disasters within Nature that result from it, large-scale arson in the Western states and provinces, biological weaponry, false flags being used as a rationale for armed invasions—these and other crimes are well known to many working in news media and entertainment, and anyone willing to look beneath the surface.

Still they remain mum, as even mentally planning to speak out via a mainstream platform can prove fatal, as many have found out.

Yet you are aware that these obvious channels of information (and disinformation) are not the only way humanity could ever learn the truth of what the Earth has been experiencing. Alternative media has grown stronger and found many new outlets over the last decade.

While you would love for the media to shake off its corporate chains and speak Truth on a daily basis, that is not where true freedom lies.

Beyond that, human beings are increasingly connecting etherically now, via what some call "the inner-net." They are connecting telepathically and intuitively with people and events around the world and with the Earth Herself, increasingly sensing when something significant is happening or about to happen. Feelings, words, or images will pop up in their heart-mind that inform them of events before the news does—or before the mainstream news can cover it up.

The current generation of children and youth are particularly empathic. Hiding things from them is getting increasingly harder to do. This is one reason why the AI [artificial intelligence] agenda is more pronounced now, though much of its presence is being mitigated or deactivated by higher dimensional beings who are assisting humanity, as well as the sentient Light particles reaching the Earth now.

Motivation for increasing their AI schema has been high amongst the old controllers. They have for many years concentrated on being able to artificially implant false ideas that do not spring naturally from a particular group or individual, yet which feel to be their own thoughts and impulses.

If you are wondering which is stronger—the increased intuitive knowing humanity is experiencing now, or the AI implants—we would say, you know this already! You are aware that the nanoparticles and the computerized forms of control behind them are failing even as we speak. Meanwhile, humanity's evolvement and expanded experience in this Universe continues to Ascend higher at every moment.

You have also entered the new era, known by its Hindu name of the Sat Yuga[2]. And so the Light coming in to the planet is not only a support to your Ascension journey. It is literally assisting in healing you of those intentional blockages thrown in your way for millennia. In doing so, it is expanding your mental and physical capability, consciousness, and social development.

When you speak of the Peace and prosperity of this new era you are now entering, *think of it as beginning within.*

It is a Joyful thing indeed for all to have a home, and nutritious food that is pure and fresh, medical care that is holistic and free of charge, equal say in matters of community and nation, and a truly free, honest, and independent press. Yet those outer situations, as positive as they are, are not the crux of the matter.

It is central to each of your journeys now, to know who you are at this time of accelerated development. So that while you would love for the media to fully awaken, shake off its corporate chains, and speak Truth on a daily basis, that is not where true freedom lies.

---

[2] The Sat Yuga is the age of reality over that of illusion—*sat* being pure or truthful reality, and *yuga* being an age or era. One website defines *sat* as "uncreated, indivisible and indistinguishable . . . the essential nature of the universal, supreme reality, the ultimate and the highest state." [From "The Meaning and Concept of Sat in Hinduism," https://www.hinduwebsite.com/hinduism/concepts/sat.asp.]

True freedom for every child, woman, and man lies in their own inner Knowing and intuitive, high-heart ability. That includes their ability to tap into any large-scale situation happening anywhere in the world that is relevant to their path, without creating an energetic intrusion. Some call that kind of knowing psychic ability—an understanding that takes place on a deep level, where Truth can only be experienced and known inwardly.

Your own beautiful, brilliant Light shines far stronger and speaks far louder than any newscast you are likely to hear.

This trait does not belong solely to those with "unusual gifts and abilities." We speak of something far greater. And that is the kind of evolvement, and the kind of planetary atmosphere, that make it increasingly harder for anyone to lie about anything. It is the form of inner connection that pulls humanity out of duality and into unity consciousness.

This is the world you are not only stepping into, but actively creating. You assist in dissolving the old system of mind control and extreme censorship whenever you share what you yourself have come to know from trusted, independent sources—or better yet, what you sense from your own inner sight and intuitive inner knowing.

Many are beginning, for example, to release partisan allegiances, feeling that in most countries, none of the major political parties are to be entirely trusted. That they are in fact corporations run by more powerful, secret corporations, and a secluded elite who have no interest in extending full rights to the masses. They are seeing that most, though not all, politicians are likewise either corrupt or threatened into submission by the ruling elite.

Given that, it is easy to see that the time for loyalty to one political party or another has well passed, and that the time for individual declaration of freedoms, on behalf of all of humanity, has finally arrived.

As that unfolds, be the truth you desire to hear!

Speak your truth when you can without alienating others, and without shutting out their opinions and ideas. In a few years' time, you will see how your own understanding of life was limited and small compared to what it will have become. You will be glad you had compassion for those who had no choice but to lie, to save not only their own lives, but that of their loved ones.

Your own beautiful, brilliant Light shines far stronger and speaks far louder than any newscast you are likely to hear. So place your focus there, and on that beautiful moment when Captain Ashtar will show up on every screen to announce NESARA's full enactment. Then trouble yourself no more, regarding the constrictions and fabrications of the *au regime*.

That day is done, and a new one dawns bright. You are that Sun you yearn to see break over the far horizon.

As our friend songwriter once said, "And *that's* reality."

4

On Viruses, Jabs, and Coming Into Your Power

What are your thoughts on Covid-19, vaccines, getting vaccinated, wearing a mask, natural immunity, mandatory vaccines, and vaccine cards?

If you were on Earth now with the knowledge you have, what would you do to protect yourself? It seems everyone has lost their minds over this.

* * *

What is the real impact on human life from the jab, compared to any other vaccine? Is it truly harmful? If so, is it any more harmful than the other multitudes of harmful exposures we already endure DAILY (5G spectrum, fluoridated water, air pollution, processed food and food additives, artificial colors, chemtrails, water pollution, lead poisoning, dangerous substances in prescribed medications, etc.).

In other words, how survivable is the jab, by comparison? Is Covid-19 as deadly as reported? If not, what is causing the hospitalizations and deaths?

If Covid-19 is harmful, is the jab truly an effective protection?

We have been asked many questions on these issues. Not surprisingly, as so many intuitively feel that the virus and the "jab" as it is called represent a sort of dividing line between Earth life as they have known it, and Earth life as it is currently.

For one, understand that your environment is already full of toxins that should not be there, as the second questioner points out. These have been, for the most part, slow-acting poisons. The virus and accompanying jab represent an accelerated form of toxification of human life.

Beyond the physical aspects of this assault and desire to control, there have also been numerous forms of mental programming, energetic entrainment, and spiritual containment. This is not a new occurrence. For centuries, these have been used to "inform and educate" humanity on what you are meant to accept as real or necessary.

What you are now seeing is the largest accelerated action yet taken on the part of the self-proclaimed authorities, in which the greater good is claimed as the reason for forced, or nearly forced, compliance with one requirement or another.

The latest forms of social control—the masks, the physical distancing, the RNA modifier "jab" mandates—are similar to other forms of social fracturing and panic-spreading. They are escalated forms of very old tactics. For some, the current situation seems more subtle than direct civilian warfare, yet it is that. It is an intentionally stepped up, direct form of mental and physical control. It was created out of the desperation that your former planetary controllers are feeling at present.

For years now they have been noting the powerfully undeniable signs of spiritual awakening of both planet and populace. They have seen the rising resonance of the Earth, and the revolutions stirring in human consciousness. As they have done in other centuries, the current configurations of the stars and planets, and the activities of your Sun Sol, lend their energies to a complete dissolving of the old oppressive systems, and into the creation of new and empowering ones. The old crowd are also seeing human DNA developing to higher levels, hence the mRNA injection meant to "redesign" (downgrade) humanity genetically.

As we have stated elsewhere, the nanoparticles in the serum are part of an operating system that, once fully rooted in the human body and brain, is designed to progressively control human beings remotely.

This is a direct violation of humanity's free will, and of the sacred organic human construct, on a mass level. Other toxins and parasites have also been included, to confuse and drastically downgrade the body's immune system.

Things would not have moved to such an extreme so quickly, were the Hour of Truth not upon you.

This is mass destruction, similar to the willful degrading of Mother Gaia's body, and the intentional disruption of the planetary climate. The illness and the deaths are real. The causes have not been revealed to the masses.

We are aware that all of this sounds exceedingly dire, and we do not say any of this to push anyone into further upset regarding the direction that Earth life is going in. Far from it!

We wish you to know that this agenda will not be successful, though we are aware that many have already fallen ill or died due to the illness, or the toxicity of this injection and other shots labeled as vaccines. Though this injection is particularly toxic, your race is being assisted on all levels.

And so we ask that you move beyond the obvious—the appearance of the moment—and consider that things would not have moved to such an extreme so quickly, were the Hour of Truth not upon you.

Regarding what is survivable, we would say, that is up to each individual's life plan, and what they will or will not allow or agree to on a higher level. Clearly, none of you came into third dimensional life because it was a balanced, fair, just, easygoing place to be. You decided well ahead of time, before incarnating

On Viruses, Jabs, and Coming Into Your Power

into each Earth life, that you desired to climb the steepest mountain possible in terms of experience, for maximum opportunity for growth.

And so you planned one Earth life after another, including being born into the current place on Earth's timeline, where the stakes feel the highest, one might say, that they ever have. You have also come in with definite Earth missions. These were designed to inspire other Light Bringers, help heal the planet from millennia of destruction, and lift the overall vibration of Earth and humanity further into Ascension.

You also desired to simply be here, so as not to miss a minute of the excitement of what is occurring now. Which is nothing less than the liberation of a planet and by extension, an entire galaxy.

We will speak on the assistance you are receiving, and endeavor to answer these questions more directly now, as they naturally feel quite pressing to you. We assure you, much good is occurring that you cannot yet see, though you may sense it. We would focus on that Lightwork as the only actual reality at this time.

Were you to view the situation on your planet now from our viewpoint, you would realize that far from having reason to despair, you have great reason to celebrate the beauty of the empowerment you are now and will continue to claim, all the way home to your complete freedom.

The real impact of "the jab," is that some are using its presence and their refusal to accept it as a kind of dividing line. They see it as a time to release themselves for good from the old agenda. While some who willingly take the shots are unconsciously using it as a way to remain in third dimensional life, they are nevertheless being given the chance to move up vibrationally.

All are also being offered forms of energetic assistance that will help nullify the damaging effects of the serum and other toxins.

You have heard of human life described as a hologram—that the Universe itself is holographic by nature—and that what you see around you at any one moment in space-time is simply an image based on energetic vibration. And so this may solve the mystery as to why some folks who never seem to stress about money or health tend to bounce back easily after an apparent loss, while others, no matter how hard they work to improve their lives, seem bound to tough circumstances. Some call this the Law of Attraction, and in many cases it is.

Yet much of your experience goes well beyond that now.

As Creator gods and goddesses, you are all of you constantly creating the reality you live in—both your own daily lives, and your planetary conditions.

You may not feel to be particularly powerful in that respect, and may spend your day feeling a bit done in from what you see around you or hear in news reports, and feel inwardly at times. Yet this does not in any way diminish your Creator capability.

You are still creating, simply in an unconscious way. And sadly for all of us who watch from the perspective of your greater selves, you are some days creating from a vibration of feeling to not be in control of what is happening to you, your loved ones, your community, your world.

Now, what happens when a person feels to have no agency in their lives, as so many have been feeling these last few years?

Clearly, this is the rockier path. One must then use vital life energy to face down what feel to be insurmountable odds, while "hoping for the best" and "waiting till it all blows over." This is a highly passive way of living, and weakens your sense of empowerment.

You who came forward at this time chose to know increasing levels of your ability to transform and transmute even the darkest of Earth life situations. In that plan, you required that those of us in the higher realms lend you our support, our wisdom, our Love—and ordered us not to launch a rescue mission.

Yet in moments of passivity and feelings of helplessness, you may indeed be waiting if not to be rescued, then for someone or something to give you a tremendous step up. That is understandable, as you have received so much information about the blessings NESARA's enactment will bring, and are connecting with your star families more often now.

On Viruses, Jabs, and Coming Into Your Power

And so you look to one event or presence or another, if not as a rescue, then as a seminal moment that supports what you have been working toward.

Take a moment to image the powerful Light pouring onto the planet, healing all touched by any illness, injury, or toxin.

Yet the idea of waiting for someone more powerful to assist you is in fact a construct the old power structure gave you.

You do not operate this way on a soul level. On a soul level, each of you knows your own power. You know that you are not only creating your own story in this great hologram, but are powerful enough to create your planet's story along with it.

For this apparently gigantic task, you have powerful tools. One of them is your own intuitive, utterly natural, co-Creative power to imagine. To visualize, which is to conceive. That skill has been scoffed at for thousands of years as "wishful thinking." It may seem to be the opposite of dealing with an issue head-on. The idea being that all action "must" be done in masculine, outer terms.

Part of you may reason that if you do not possess the abilities of a superhero (though you do), then why call yourself empowered? Why feel as if you are strong enough to vanquish any foe?

Take a moment right now, to image the powerful, sentient, golden Light pouring onto the planet. See it reaching and healing all touched by any illness, injury, or toxin. Then image the Earth Herself becoming healed and renewed in gentle ways.

You are within that Light and all its higher intent. It is not separate from you.

You may also wish to image all wildfires stopped before they begin. All floods averted, all droughts quenched by gentle rains. All children fed, educated, lovingly watched over while offered empowering support and caring guidance. All women elevated to receiving the respect the Divine Feminine accords all, and calls forth from all now.

Image all weaponry of any kind falling silent, and being utterly eradicated, as all realize, *There is no need for war of any kind.*

Image not only the arrest, containment, and tribunals of those who have wreaked havoc on the planet for so long, but their continuing evolvement as they regain their souls from the dark realms. And see those realms flooded with Light as well, at levels they can integrate.

Image higher healing technologies emerging, alongside the higher energies you are now receiving. Your Sun is particularly active in this respect, as he no longer lives within the constraints once put upon him by the previous Universal era.

Hold an image each day of your entire Earth held lovingly inside the Violet Transmuting Flame of Saint Germain.

And most vitally, image all of humanity saying with one voice, "No more! Be gone!" to this last dark, desperate agenda. Image all of humanity saying as one voice, "We choose to stand in the Light." Do this, though you are aware that many feel they are doing the right thing by willingly following false authority, and willingly supporting the false information they are given.

Image them blending with their higher selves in that moment. See them awakening to the beauty of the New Earth, and evolving into the New Human, who intuitively sees through all delusion, all lies and manipulations of any kind, and will not tolerate them.

Image this each day with all the Joy, inner strength, and Love for your planet that is within you. Or simply image each day your entire Earth, held lovingly inside the Violet Transmuting Flame of Saint Germain.

This transmuting power is yours to use at any time. Use it for your own life, for whatever you wish to heal and transform, until that experience transmutes to a far higher vibrational level. And use it for your Earth and Her people, and all living things upon Her.

Certainly, image NESARA being enacted, with Captain Ashtar and the Ascended Masters joining in for the announcing of NESARA's full enactment on every screen on the Earth, simultaneously. And of course, image the ships landing and the celebrations occurring all over the planet as soul families are reunited.

Call all of this forth! Hold it in your heart-mind. Celebrate it! Expect it!

This is your Earth life vision, all of it powerful in intent and outcome.

Some days you will need to hold these images or the feelings they stir within you, even when they seem not enough to change Earth life. In those moments, call out to Archangel Michael and his Legions of Light to assist at an even greater level than they are now, including offering you greater levels of courage. They are more than happy to assist.

You have asked to know the true impact on human life brought about by this virus, which is indeed real, though intentionally created and lied about by a corrupt scientific system. Its effects have also been artificially enhanced by dark technologies. Most assuredly, the losses there are real.

Yet understand that much is being mitigated, as much as you are all permitting on a higher level. You are actively calling forth great assistance now, in empowered cooperation with Earth-based and galactic Forces of Light, the Angelic legions, and your own souls. That last element being the most crucial here.

We cannot "save" your planet for you. Yet you are accomplishing this already, by making active use of that Light which daily falls upon your Earth and flows into your lives in ways that awaken you all the more potently to your own Creator aspect.

That is your own Divinity, and your own Beautiful forms of Peace, of Truth. This is a power that can only flow from within, moving further into the Light in celebration of the All That Is.

This is who you are, friends! Not a conquered people on a conquered planet, but a community of gods and goddesses, creating together an expression of your highest dream.

Know this, and claim it fully. Though we cannot do this for you, we cheer you on at every moment. Our Love for you, and our great appreciation of your bravery and your vision, is constant and real.

Namaste, dear ones! You are more powerful than you could know.

5

On Staying in Love, Joy, and Wonder

My question is about maintaining my connection to God, my fellow Earthlings, and all the magical aspects of existence I've been learning about over the past few years.

Though I continue to read, take classes, and learn in order to maintain and continue my expansion of Love, I snap back to fear and smallness as quick as a rubber band.

I have to try so hard to stay high and in touch with Love and joy and wonder. If I'm not continually putting effort in, I slide back, and life feels hard and dark and scary.

Something tells me there's an easier way, and I'm hoping you can help me with that.

This is an excellent question, particularly in this time! The false old Earth systems are doing all they can to resist the higher Light now. This is so.

Yet the human desire to flow into the Presence of higher Light and stay there, has never been greater!

This conundrum is not always easy to take. It is possible to desire real growth, and to focus on expanding one's energies to resonate with Divine Love. Yet there are times when the requirements of life now feel too dense and heavy to bear, and sometimes frightening.

We would say, that this is a part of the steeper aspect of your path, and the paths of many millions of others now. You are realizing that you came in to this Earth life with the intention to grow in ways you had not grown in the past.

You came in to overcome the old pitfalls. To forgive old grievances, and end old soul contracts. To release old etheric influences that try to pull you away from your own higher instincts. You desired to know and demonstrate the pure Love of Divinity in everyday life.

And yet, the resistance can indeed be great, within as well as without.

Know that the impulse to weigh and measure where you are spiritually is part of the old order. You will notice a far lighter feeling in your own mind and heart-space, as you release judgment of "how I'm doing" as far as how pure and loving your heart-mind and general mood are at any one time.

Release that habit! Whenever it comes up, smile at it. Go beyond it. The shifts you are experiencing at present are remaking every cell of your being. Allow yourself moments of tiredness, sadness, or insecurity, without judgment. Be kind; be encouraging, as you would be to anyone.

Many struggle now, yet have their eye on a brighter day, dawning deep within them. And so we would ask, *Who are you in your most brilliant moments?* Those moments when you help a stranger who is struggling in some way, and see the look of relief on their face.

The times when you sit with a loved one who is struggling, and note the purity and nobility of their path, holding that energy in your heart as they spill out how sad and confused they feel. In those moments you are not rushing to remedy the situation, but simply listening, and making room for their own inner Wisdom to come forward. A great gift to them!

Who are you in those moments when you laugh joyfully at a comic, or a friend's humor (or your own)?

Who are you when you gaze at the night sky and smile and greet your soul family who are in the ships, to tell them you love them, and will see them soon?

Or in those moments when you feel you cannot fully enough express your appreciation for another's brilliance, or teaching ability, or kindness that never expects to be repaid?

You are, in those moments, your true self—your Angelic aspect, who never seeks to define itself by ego. That aspect who would never dream of scoring itself on how well it's "measuring up" to some ideal the mind dreamt up long ago.

Basking in the pure Light of Divine Love, you would only think to give Thanks and Appreciation that the path is never-ending. That it can never be finished, so long as there is more to experience, more to experiment with. Something even greater to be or to meet, or to experience.

You would only think to say, "Thank you" to a Universe which never seeks to judge. That All That Is presence which gives back over and over as you give to yourself and others, with full knowledge that Joy can only expand, though it may feel to be asleep at times. Expansion and outer expression are its true nature, its most favorite moment!

To catch on, to magnify, to explore and do more—this is what Joy seeks, and which Love does naturally, without containment.

Your vulnerability is the sensitivity with which you perceive a New Earth being born.

You will not feel Joyful while focusing on the days when you feel to have lost the shine of your own brilliance—days when the path feels to be all uphill. This is part of the experience you came in for. Though you may feel it is a departure from that plan, it is an integral part of it.

If fear or feelings of smallness move in at times, allow them without judgment. Observe where they seem to have come from, without needing to fix or change how you are feeling or thinking at first. In truth, you are a reflecting pool for the beauty and power of the higher realms.

Yet you are also in a human body that is many days tired, uncertain, and most assuredly, trained to react to much stimuli as a potential threat.

Yet this vulnerability is your goldmine, dear one, and must be treated as such. This is the sensitivity with which you perceive a New Earth being born, and a new level of consciousness being created, which not all are yet fully aware of.

This is not an indication that you are not strong enough spiritually, but that you are Spirit itself, and are experiencing what you came in to experience, which is the release of density you feel some days. Not because it defines you, but because *it flows through you on its way to being transmuted to something much higher in vibration.*

Of course you do not want to be a channel for dense emotion indefinitely, nor is that your main role. Yet understand that in those times when your life feels more difficult than you are comfortable with, you are not losing anything, nor failing anyone. You are doing the job you came in to do: to Ascend your own experience of density, thereby assisting in the Ascension of the planet by anchoring in Her your own growth and expansion, and all the Light your soul can lend to the process.

Most assuredly, life can feel hard and dark and scary, as you say, in these times when the darkness is coming up, to be transmuted into something higher. Or dissolved back into raw energy, and fully released from the Earth and all human systems.

Ascension does not mean that all will stroll about smiling with ease and Joy, and never a problem in the world. It means, for many millions, the opposite of that some days. The pain of this is too much for some, and they have left their physical body one way or another, due to the pressure of releasing and transmuting what they and so many others have carried for so long. Currently, the pain must be felt first, before the shift can come.

Often, it is not a pleasant process. And yet—there is no judgment. Not for those who choose to leave, nor for those who suffer some days, feeling that the weight of this Transformation is simply too much.

Rather than feel that falling into the hard-and-scary energy is a sign of loss of awareness, let it key you in to greater awareness of what you have come in to heal.

It is so that you and humanity are not pirouetting gracefully through the toughest climb a human being can take on. This does not make the miracle of your evolvement any less remarkable, or less beautiful! Look at the years of intense training a dancer must take on, in order to make near-impossible movements look effortless!

Likewise, the modern artist may splash paint upon the canvas in a way that feels to them to be a demonstration of sheer anger or loss. Yet the outcome can be a thing of beauty for all those who admire the honesty of it, who see a resolution—some hidden grace the artist did not at first know was there.

You are the artist, dear one. You are the one to release whatever you are feeling in a way that is positive and alive—through music or movement, journaling, or sharing with another. Through spending time in Nature, in which you see that even the perfection of the changing seasons must bring the barren trees and freezing cold of winter, and the blistering Sun of summer.

You are this, as well as the perfection of spring and its cheerful awakening. Observe how water flows. There may be a great splash when it hits a rock or other encumbrance, yet it still flows easily up and over or around the rocks, because it is the miracle of flow itself.

There is also within you that ability to flow. To return to the Joy of moving with life rather than against it. Yet that will not come from "thinking" your way there. Or by trying to force your heart-space to "lighten up."

You will need to develop everyday practices that assist you in moving into a calm Peacefulness.

You speak of reading and studying so as to move forward spiritually, and we would say that certainly that is a support to your path. Yet the Peacefulness, Joy, and experience of Divine Love that you seek will not come purely from knowledge or mental focus.

Move into the heart-space each morning, before you fully begin your day, by going into meditation or visualization, or chanting a mantra that speaks to whatever vibration you prefer to move into. There is much online that can assist you with this, and many guided meditations that can bring you to where you begin the day with a focus on calm, rather than a haphazard forward movement that is all about what needs "to get done" that day.

This early morning attention to centering your energies on your higher self presence stands on the fact that the Universe always awaits your focus and attention. That focus is the same as *a request and a requirement* that the Universe and your higher self assist you in flowing with the higher energies as your set point—the place you meet the day from.

You are then directing your mind and emotions to flow at a higher vibrational level each day, rather than hoping that no dense thought or feeling will decide your day for you.

In addition to not judging your denser thoughts and emotions, we would also encourage you to seek assistance and support for healing or releasing whatever feels heavy to you. Keep in mind that much of what you feel is not who you really are. Much of this is based on forms of trauma from this and other lives, buried deep within your psyche and spirit.

Much old pain is coming to the surface now at this time of unprecedented Light, to finally be healed. And nearly all persons on the planet also deal with energy and entity interferences, which can be cleared from your energies with specific clearing processes and by skilled energy workers.

Rather than feel that falling into the hard-and-scary energy is a sign of loss of awareness, let it key you in to even greater awareness of what you have come in to finally heal. See it as some part of you asking to be fully felt, and finally released.

It is asking for more Love, not more fear or judgment.

You are yourself a microcosm of all you seek.

You have at your disposal wonderful forms of energy healing, and practices such as Tapping (Emotional Freedom Technique), journaling or speaking with a spiritually aware counselor, speaking with your Spirit team, meditation, chanting a mantra, a daily yoga or Tai Chi practice, working with affirmations and visualizations, and live or recorded energy clearings. Experiment a bit, and see which practices feel to be drawing you in, and which you feel to benefit from the most. This is highly individual, and can vary over time.

Early on in the day, it is vital now to move into the heart-space, to speak to your Spirit team, and to call in the support you require at this time. Know that your vulnerabilities and your need for healing quiet, and alone time, are as sacred to your path and Earth mission as the moments of Joy or enlightenment so lauded in spiritual circles.

Honor your path. All of it!

It is not as Divine as you are. Yet it aspires to be. Be kind, and be generous to yourself now. Do your best to image and if possible, to feel the presence of countless beautiful Light Beings who are all around you. Those who never sleep as they watch over you and lend you loving support—and the wisdom and healing you call in, insist on, rejoice in, expect.

All is well, in this and so many other ways. You need never worry about your connection to Creator God/Goddess or the All That Is, and your fellow Earthlings.

You could not be other than constantly and perfectly interconnected with all of Life.

Nor could you be separate from Divinity, for you are the perfect expression of it. You are yourself a microcosm of all you seek, though you do not yet recognize yourself as being that.

And know that the shadows too have their role, and in their own way, seek the Light.

For all of us who see your desire to return to your highest aspect—yes, we see your Divinity. And for us, *that* is true Joy, in so many ways.

6

On the Power of Your Presence

As a Lightworker and sensitive soul, I'm feeling the need right now more than ever to rest and prepare mentally and physically, but not be afraid in my preparation of what is to come.

How do we best carry this inner knowing through our day-to-day life, and the minutia of what occurs each day?

How do we help our friends and families when we are not to be rescuers, but turned more towards healing and helping ourselves? I have noticed the feeling of needing to mostly turn inward right now, making sure my energy does not deplete.

What is the most important action or thing for Lightworkers to focus on at this time?

And how do I continue to lean into the belief that I am here to spread that Light? That I'm meant to just hold the vibration within me, emanate it, and just be?

Is that all it takes at this time?

Let us begin with your statement about resting and preparing in all ways for what is to come. For that is, in a sense, based on a supposition, such as, "This might happen in a month or a year," or "Predictions are that _____ may be happening soon. So much is in upheaval!"

There is no saying what is to come, outside of a broader picture of the planet regaining Her sovereignty. And what is currently with you is not only sufficient for your path, but all you need deal with at any one time in your life.

What you imagine to be a linear or pre-determined timeline is neither. Much is shifting so quickly, that to say you must prepare for the future and yet not fall into fear, is nearly a moot point.

All times are Now. Not only is the present moment your main focal point, but, as mentioned earlier, it is the only moment you need ever deal with.

Certainly you will feel your own vulnerability now, and your need to rest from the rigors of the present moment. Yet release all future-oriented concerns. Your own tiredness from the stresses and unexpected "stretching" of your own resources will be enough. There is no need to carry with you throughout the day the mental reminder that you are traveling a demanding path that might only get worse.

You will need to replenish your inner resources in quiet time each day. Your own experience has shown you that. There is no need to think of future events as stretching you even further. Give power to your ability to face that which is already at hand.

Offer yourself the kind of supportive Love you would offer a small child entering a new world.

Life on Earth now requires that each person heal or dissolve all energy blocks and old wounding, throughout the Ascension process. So that rather than "rest and prepare" we would say, "rest and *repair*," as the highest form of self-care are required now. Release the assumption that everything will get even more difficult than it has been the last few years.

Expect great change. But change that tilts the planetary experience and vibration to as high a level as humanity can withstand and still exist, as all move into increasingly higher

On the Power of Your Presence

levels of enlightenment. Into increasingly higher levels of Love for yourselves, the Earth, and one another.

Meet the present moment in a place of calm. Keep a calm detachment from outer events, which do not determine your life unless you allow them to.

You ask how best to help friends and family, when you are not be their rescuers—an excellent point! That is indeed not what you are here for, though you have been trained to expect to be a rescuer or a savior in many situations. Those roles are not helpful, in the end.

Many an Ascended Master has attempted to lift the vibration of humanity to a higher level. Yet none has succeeded in lifting it beyond what humans as a mass consciousness were willing to allow.

And so, yes—one is left viewing the morass. The madness of life on a contentious planet of extreme polarities in climate, income, politics, military action, social structures, consciousness. Yet yours is now a planet ever reaching toward increasing levels of Peaceful Abundance. And in this era, Her people concur, in increasing numbers, that that must be achieved for the good of all.

It is so that healing and helping oneself is the unavoidable path now. Turn inward and retreat to a quiet place when the Transformation you and so many others desire catches up with you. It will demand more rest, and a deeper wisdom than your conscious mind will automatically reach for. For that, you must tap into higher resources than what you find around you, and offer yourself the kind of supportive Love you would offer a small child entering a new world.

It is that, believe it or not, that must be at the top of your list of things to do each day.

Not saving the planet, or saving humanity. Not "saving" anyone in the old Earth sense. When we speak of being a Light on the path of others, we speak of your example. Of transmitting higher Light with your very being. And of inspiring and empowering others via your very presence. Your belief in them and your confidence that they are on the right path, or finding that. Not doing the job for them, which would be impossible.

Of course the very young or elderly, and those who have disabilities, injuries, illnesses—these persons require obvious support. Yet when you speak of assisting friends and family who are utterly capable, we would say, be careful that your empathy does not move your energy into theirs. Be aware that you may be unconsciously leaning forward into their energies, taking on the weight of their life experiences. Or lending them your life energies, feeling this will assist them.

You cannot continue to carry your own unresolved wounding without creating a great gap between where you desire to be and where you are now.

Many empaths carry extra body weight, and you can probably guess why. Certainly many carry it as a layer of protection between them and the world. The many conflicting vibrations of the world are hard for them to process or shield themselves from, in addition to their own past trauma. In some cases, the subconscious holds added weight on the body as a guarantee that fewer people will find them attractive (as is the case with many women sexually abused in childhood), thereby lowering the potential threat of abuse. Or their subconscious may reason that no one can harm them physically, now they are no longer small and vulnerable.

Be aware that you cannot carry others' life energies, or continue to carry your own unresolved wounding, without creating a great gap between where you desire to be in life, and where you are now.

Many already live in that place of discomfort, and are finding it close to unbearable. And so, we encourage all to deal with the trauma they carry. As you heal, you light the way for many thousands to follow. With your example and your inner Light shining in a way that only a healed person can shine, you will be empowering them to face their own pains and losses, and to seek healing for them.

So perhaps the most important thing for Light Bringers to do now, is to move along the path of learning and Being in the highest way possible, in loving ways that honor your unique makeup and your unique path.

We encourage all to seek quiet time, and time in Nature. To have a quiet meditation time each day. To seek out some form of exercise that is joyful to you, and some form of creative expression. And to support all of the unhealed aspects of spirit and psyche that are coming to the surface now, however you are able to.

Many modalities of energy healing are available now, and you are also able to do much on your own. These practices can include working with scripts and videos for Tapping (Emotional Freedom Technique) that address whatever issues you are facing now, as well as listening to energy clearings, automatic writing in which you channel your child self or past life selves, or simply speaking with your Spirit team of guides, Angelic guardians, and higher self. There are many options.

See what calls to you, and what seems to assist you best in releasing the heaviness of so many lives lived on a low dimensional Earth and other planets.

Again, we encourage all to daily image themselves being cleansed and transformed by the Violet Transmuting Flame of Saint Germain. Each day, hold the image of the entire Earth in that cool Violet Flame. In that beautiful fire, all old frequencies are moving to a higher level, and the density and shadows are lightening by the moment.

Offering encouragement and kindness to others, with respect for their path, even if it seems very divergent from your own, will also be powerfully helpful. In those moments, you extend Love and support to those parts of your own spirit that have been split off and forgotten for a very long time.

In your visualizations for the Earth now, as you blaze the Violet Flame, call forth the full power of Divine Justice—the Goddesses of Justice, of Freedom, of Unity, of Divine Rebirth and Renewal. All of these beautiful beings have held different titles and names over the millennia, yet all live in service to the Light, and to the Oneness of All That Is. All will hear and come forth to assist your planet as you call to them.

Likewise, call upon Archangel Michael and his Angelic Legions of Light! Ask them to sweep clear all the lower vibrations that feed corruption on the planet, throughout all militaries, all governmental and para-governmental agencies, all corporations and corporate structures (including all organized religion), and all persons involved in these, in any way.

This imagery, and giving over the weight of what humanity experiences now, and what you yourself experience now, will not take much time in your day. Yet these will help you realize at a deep level that you are assisted now by all the powers of the higher realms. That you are never alone in your journey. And that all has higher meaning that at the moment, you may only sense and not quite see.

Yet your capacity for Love, for Joy, for being at Peace in the fullest sense—all of this, and the powerful transmission of Light that your presence provides—that is the great gift of your life on this planet! You offer these in addition to the Earth mission you are fulfilling, without yet fully knowing what that is.

Many days, that is all it takes. Much depends on your individual path, and the learning and restoring of your authentic self and soul presence in your body. Yet as you are able to offer your own life as a powerful demonstration of higher Light—what could be better than this?

No arguments needed, no debates or persuasions so that others view life as you do. No rescues or worries. None of it necessary, as they are swept up in the power of your presence and the beauty of your unconditional Love and acceptance of them.

This has transformed worlds, dear ones! And yes, it is enough!

7

On the Enactment of NESARA Law

I have not heard anything about NESARA lately. Is that still supposed to happen, or has it been "tabled" indefinitely? What is its current status?

NESARA law has not been tabled, and steps toward its enactment are continuously in the works.

We will explain, for those not yet aware, that with the help of the Ashtar Command, NESARA (the National Economic Security and Reformation Act) was quietly voted on and passed by the United States Congress, and signed into law in October of 2000 by then US President William Clinton.

It has not yet been fully enacted, yet you will see signs of its impending enactment in many areas of human life— breakthrough moments in technology, consciousness, and human rights that seem to herald its forthcoming announcement.

Let us look at a few of the provisions of this Earth-changing law, and the ways in which human life will be transformed once it comes fully into place.

Once fully enacted, NESARA:

- Erases all credit card, mortgage, and other bank debt, due to illegal banking and government activities
- Abolishes the Internal Revenue Service and all income tax
- Creates a 14% flat rate sales tax on all new, nonessential items, as revenue for the government—food and medicine will not be taxed, nor will used items such as older homes
- Increases benefits to seniors and those with disabilities
- Returns constitutional law to all courts and legal matters
- Requires new presidential and congressional elections within 120 days after NESARA's announcement
- Monitors elections and prevents illegal election activities of special interest groups
- Creates a new US Treasury rainbow currency—one backed by gold, silver, and platinum precious metals
- Forbids the sale of American birth certificate records as chattel property bonds by the US Department of Transportation
- Begins a new US Treasury banking system in alignment with Constitutional law
- Eliminates the Federal Reserve system
- Ends all aggressive US government military actions worldwide
- Establishes Peace throughout the world—US troops will be brought home from around the world as Peace is declared; in alignment with the Constitution, there will be no standing armies, and that will be permanently observed
- Releases enormous sums of money for humanitarian purposes
- Enables the release of thousands of suppressed technologies currently being withheld from the public under the guise of national security, including free energy devices, antigravity devices, and sonic healing machines

NESARA's precepts will apply to all nations, as best serves each culture's individuality. The greatest changes that NESARA law will bring, however, are not the outer shifts in human life, but the inner shifts.

In other words, NESARA will bring with it vibrational gifts that empower human beings to see the very great forms of agency they have—what they are able to create, heal, change, or dissolve in their individual lives and communities.

You are already seeing NESARA consciousness breaking through amongst those whose Earth mission involves anchoring NESARA vibrations into Earth life. Many of these people are involved in bringing forth forms of free energy, sustainable building materials that are simple and easy to use for construction of homes, schools, businesses, and other buildings. Many are involved in healing people, animals, plants, and the environment energetically rather than through the very constricted forms of medicine now known to the mainstream.

Others are involved in lifting spiritual growth issues out of the confines of traditional religion. It is time that humanity realized both the powerful expanse of the human soul and the vulnerability of it, after centuries of dense third dimensional living. This is the journey of reaching beyond dogma to spiritual reality. The focus will be opening to the power of spiritual experience and inner knowing, rather than rote learning of false belief systems.

These have outrun their uses in Earth life, though some will still hold meaning for many, and those persons will not be denied that which is important to them on a personal level. Yet many will find that they will seek new forms of spiritual growth and expression. The higher energies that will flow freely throughout the Earth during and after NESARA's announcement to the world will assist in this.

Do not cease in giving Thanks for this breakthrough moment that will transform not only the planet, but each of your individual lives.

Though the above changes will begin in the United States, they will soon extend to all other nations around the world, till the entire globe is released from the old, very dark governing structures.

It may at times feel as if NESARA has been put on permanent hold. And yet—do you see the disruption happening upon the Earth now?

Do you see the drastic shifts occurring in politics—the demonstrations and demands for human sovereignty on a raft of issues? You can no doubt see the shifts occurring in medicine, as people require more holistic care that addresses the whole person, and in nontoxic ways. And in education, as many now opt to home-school their children, in order to more fully guide what and how their children are learning.

You also see shifts in media—look at the power of independent media now. The independent news broadcasts, self-published books and websites, independently produced podcasts, music, video, and film—all of it self-propelled by group and individual voices that would not be silenced by the old power structure.

We do not say that all of this content is positive for human experience. Yet note the overall trend to self-creation and thought that runs with no submission to the old authority structure! Compared to the tight control of past eras, this is nearly miraculous.

All of these areas of independent thought, realization, growth, and action are clear proof that the spirit of NESARA is already afoot. Already present in human life, and growing stronger by the day.

This is occurring as beautiful and empowering Light from your Sun Sol is pouring onto the planet every moment, awakening human consciousness and healing and raising the vibration of Earth as never before. The combination of the two "packs a wallop" in terms of paving the way to NESARA's enactment.

For a more complete history of NESARA law, we would encourage you to seek out the Rainbow Roundtable (Faction Three White Knights') website,[3] as well as our writer's website,

---

[3] For more information on NESARA Law, go to https://www.rainbowroundtable.net/nesara-law and to https://www.ascensiontimes.com/nesara for a "NESARA Q&A" from the Collective.

and read of the fascinating background and history of this new paradigm-creating law, which will bring Earth law back into alignment with Universal law.

Remember that you have the ongoing support of the Ashtar Command. That empowered group is comprised of beings who have lived thousands, some even millions of years. They have assisted other planets in crisis, and carry with them the wisdom and knowledge required to assist Earth at this crucial moment.

Hold within yourselves not only the Joy and full realization of what lies ahead, but what is already occurring.

It was the Ashtar Command, aided by Archangel Michael and the Light Forces, and the soul of the Earth Herself, who came to support the democratic design established by Ascended Master Saint Germain. This is the basis of the NESARA's precepts, now viewed by your star families as an increasing necessity for human life.

These powerful beings serve the Light, and are consistently engaged in aiding Earth and humanity in establishing full sovereignty and an end to all tyranny, per the crystalline or *krystos* (christed) consciousness now unfolding in all areas of Earth life.

These Light Forces include several million militia members who are on the ground upon the Earth Herself, known as White Knights of the Ashtar Command. They work tirelessly to promote Earth and humanity's freedom, and to pave the way to NESARA's enactment. It is by their dedication, and the dedication of every Light Bringer on Earth, to performing the Earth mission they came in for, that we speak so positively in terms of the inevitability of NESARA's enactment.

For one, that is the timeline that Earth is now on—a far higher timeline vibrationally than the planet was on even 10 years ago. For another, if enough people hold something to be true in their vibration for a particular space-time, it must be so, and that critical mass is quickly approaching.

So do not be shy in your expectation of and celebration of NESARA's enactment! Much is unfolding behind the scenes that you do not see or hear of directly, though many of you engage with those efforts in etheric form, and contribute to them with your life energies. This is greatly appreciated and highly valued, beyond what we can say in Earth language.

And so, do not cease in giving Thanks and Appreciation for this breakthrough moment that will transform not only the planet, but each of your own individual lives! We see it unfolding even now in the etheric, opening the door to full disclosure of the extraterrestrial presence, and to your galactic families coming forward to assist in the healing and cleansing of your planet.

We also see it opening the door to Earth beings realizing that they are again a member of a Galactic Federation of other peaceful civilizations, and from there, part of an Intergalactic Confederation of Worlds.

This is only the beginning. So hold within yourselves not only the Joy and full realization of what is already unfolding, including in your own energies.

Yes, this is real. Hold as active, in the Now moment, that day when every screen holds the images of the announcement that NESARA is now fully enacted.

Expect it, and know that it is so.

And so it is!

8

On Resistance, and Stepping Up in a Time of Crisis

There are so many of us that are doers. Can you give us concrete steps or a loose map for us to take action on?

The absolute subjugation or extermination of the human population is happening at the moment, and there are many of us ready to take more action than being in resistance.

* * * * *

What are we to do, besides sticking to our beliefs and marching? Is there anything else? I know how far I am willing to go to stand up for my beliefs. I will risk it all.

I know people are waiting for God to intervene. I believe that it is time for humanity to step up and take responsibility. I cannot believe how brainwashed everyone is, but I understand that it is the choice they make.

How far will we have to go, and what is your counsel to us right now?

Both of these excellent queries address a situation that is the most immediately painful for many. They sense intuitively that the illness that has raced through most parts of the world over the last few years was not an accident.

Likewise, many have noted the very quick appearance of a medical pre-treatment that the masses have been lead to believe will protect them from becoming ill, which in fact carries its own hidden dangers.

And so, yes—this is an attempted extermination of the majority of the human race. Many in various countries have attached party politics to this scenario. We would say, lift your eyes, and look further than that. This situation is far greater than any one political party's preferences or claims. Political parties are almost always used as levers of control over hearts and minds, by the same crowd of controllers you have dealt with on this planet for thousands of years. They wear many faces.

Now, for a moment, let us look well beyond the extermination and control agenda.

Let us look at why you have come in at this time—why any Light Bearer in their right mind would come in at this time!—and how you are to process what is happening now. Which is not only a matter of dealing with the depth of dark intent against humanity. Also involved is Lady Gaia Herself, standing amidst weather manipulation, large-scale drought and arson, manufactured Earth disturbances, and so on.

In this moment, when it would appear that all is lost, you are in fact in a moment of unprecedented breakthrough.

Let us look beyond the destruction, both actual and intended, and ask why you would come in at this time carrying higher Light. You chose this time to take on the Ascension path. To evolve your consciousness to where you can see and speak with Light Beings and extraterrestrial friends, guides, and family members as easily as you would a next door neighbor. And to heal yourself, and in so doing, to assist in the healing of others, and your planet.

On Resistance, and Stepping Up in a Time of Crisis

All of that sounds to be a big enough challenge. And then, *this* happens!

Certainly you could have stayed behind in the higher realms and still assisted humanity wherever possible at this time of unparalleled challenge in human life.

As you say, Why come in now, *simply to resist the dark side's plans, and openly oppose them?*

Some forms of resistance have merit, of course. To speak one's truth, to stand in protection of others, and in protection of Life itself, is a powerful way of the Light Warrior. It takes much bravery. And it reassures many that they are not alone in their realization that much is rotten in the state of Denmark, and that human rights must be upheld.

Yet that truth-telling can also unconsciously contribute to the divisiveness that the shadow realm feeds off of. Its control depends upon people being divided against one another, while also suffering splits in their own consciousness.

Know that if you do speak out against what is being hoisted onto Earth's population at present, this is not a lost effort. Your inner passion and refusal to support what is happening now is a powerful stand. You speak in favor of all persons awakening and shaking off the shackles of many, many Earth lives in which humans have been threatened and forced into obedience of the old power structure.

Yet as valiant as all that resistance sounds, we agree that to fight what is happening is not enough.

And so for a moment, let us leave Earth. Let us visit a ship, cloaked and residing quietly above the planet.

Stand with us now, and look out the large window that shows you one side of Earth in Her nighttime beauty. Many small pinpoints of light join, illuminating the places where towns and cities are aglow with the lights of buildings, homes, and vehicles, brightening spaces that seem small from such a distance.

From this particular viewpoint, you do not see struggle, though you most assuredly sense it. Yet you do not fall prey to the depths of intense emotion. You are not in reaction. You stand as an advanced being, as an Earth human might call you, feeling a great Love for Mother Earth, without the desperation so many of Her inhabitants feel at present.

For you are also able to see the magnificence of this moment. In fact, as they say, *you would not have missed it for anything.*

The magnificence has nothing to do with the power struggle being witnessed by those who stand upon the Earth now. It has to do with the times these Earth humans live in. And this moment on Her current elevated timeline holds astounding potential for experiencing a level of grace, healing, and true inner power that humanity could have only dreamt of a century ago.

Indeed, some did dream of it! You and many others were amongst them. And so you incarnated once again, to be part of what you knew would be a time of unprecedented Light coming into the planet from your Sun Sol. That great, sentient Being of solar Light consciousness is simply passing on to you the powerful energetic waves of new Life that the Great Central Sun is beaming out to him. And your Sun will continue to do so, in ever-increasing amounts, over thousands of years.

These golden Light particles carry their own mission, and it is a mission that well outweighs the plans of the old order. Yes, you came in to witness this. To be here on Earth as these pinpoints of seemingly magical presences—many trillions of them at each moment—flow to Earth and Earth consciousness. For in this moment, when it would appear that all is lost, you are in fact in a moment of unprecedented breakthrough.

This is the moment when Earth regains Her status from lost civilization, isolated from all other civilizations, to being once again a part of the Galactic Federation of Worlds. And no small part of this, is that Her citizens are remembering their lost aspects, reclaiming their lost DNA, and rising in vibration to that of fifth dimensional beings.

You knew you could stay behind and assist energetically, yet the immediate interaction was something you would not give up.

So now, look around this highly advanced vessel you are on. Does anything there look familiar to you? The ship itself, or the crew? Are any of them old friends, or family members? Is one perhaps your twin flame?

On Resistance, and Stepping Up in a Time of Crisis

Look down—how are you dressed? Are you in another form, other than your usual Earth human shape and size? What is your role on this ship, if any?

We ask these questions, because this is the form so many of you are in while in your sleep state each night. Missions vary, and appearances vary. But all of you have had times aboard a ship of one form or another, and looked down upon the Earth, and considered or discussed Her current state of affairs with others. You have in fact done this for centuries.

Then at some point, you decided to embark upon yet another Earth journey, understanding that this particular lifetime would be the end of a long line of third dimensional lives.

Whether on a ship or in the higher realms, you knew there was work to be done on the surface of Earth, by those in human form, and holding human consciousness. You knew that you could if you wished, stay behind and assist energetically. Yet the immediate interaction with other Earth beings and the planet Herself was something you would not give up.

This was due to your great Love for Her, and for all Her beings.

You also knew no rescue mission was needed, nor could it be called for, due to the contract that Earth's people have long had with the higher realms. You knew that this would be a very immediate, on-call form of assistance. And that it would potentially draw you back into old patterns in your own consciousness that would be painful to re-experience.

Yet this is part of why you incarnated once again! You knew there were unfinished chapters to finally complete, to close for good.

If you are wondering at your sanity, in taking on so many higher directives at once, and wish to inform your higher self that they should have warned you well away from any such plan—be assured, you were indeed warned. You were told in very clear terms what this particular "away team" venture would mean, and that the wear and tear on your inner life would be at least as hard as it had been in other lives, if not plenty harder.

For in this particular Earth life, you may not undergo physical torture at the hands of government or religious authorities, or be ostracized from your family or village. Yet you knew that the pain and trauma of that from other lives would rise to be healed, forcing you to re-experience it on a deep level. You have all experienced much of the depths of the third dimensional life and vibration. You came in knowing it was time to release the old agreements and contracts, the old trauma, and the false self created to survive it all.

"All of this, to even out my past misdeeds?" you may ask. "To ensure that I Ascend as far as possible? To assist a planet that looks to be in the Her death throes one minute, and the birthing process the next? It's too much! Could no one stop me?"

No, actually. We couldn't. And that is the beauty of it. Your free will, which at this moment appears to be utterly usurped and held prisoner by the old power structure, has never been stronger, or you would not be here now.

Regarding doing more than resisting the current order, we would say, one of your greatest forms of refusal to "play" along with their dark games would be to refuse to panic, to refuse to despise or even to judge them. And to refuse to fall into despair over the circumstances of your or anyone's life.

Begin there, with that strong decision to avoid their old games of divide-and-conquer or induced fear.

Then move forward into claiming your right to a Peaceful existence, regardless of your life circumstances. That Peace will need to begin within, and again, will take a strong decision. Yet you are all capable of such. Then at some point, you will allow yourselves to move on to Joy. To those forms and levels of Abundance that are for your higher good. To Love in its many forms. To fulfillment and self-expression.

To that moment of helping Frodo throw the last ring into the fires of Mordor, and to the Joy that awaits you beyond that moment.

Your own frequency is your key out of the prison you were forced to build for yourself long ago.

Now, from an Earth viewpoint, that only sounds like more madness, because so many suffer now in a variety of strenuous circumstances, including wondering where their next meal will come from. Yet what we speak of doesn't come from your reaction to circumstance, and does not rest in what you prefer. It goes much deeper than that.

Your true gift to the Earth and Her people now, whether those you know or those who live on other continents, is to hold the vibration that All Is Well. Even though your logical mind will enjoy arguing with that, informing you that on the contrary, now would be the perfect time to panic, or at least feel very stressed.

To the logical mind, we would say, We are sorry you have been so abused. So deliberately programmed for expectation of calamity. So completely trained to overcome the higher impulses of the heart-mind, the spirt, and the soul.

We are sorry that you have been presented as the only tool by which a human can survive, outside of a few desperate prayers to some god who lives separately from you, somewhere high above, and who cannot relate to your very human situation—supposedly including even "He who came here once."

We would say to the left-brain, You have many gifts. You are wonderful at building a fire under people and encouraging them to "do" everything possible to fix an unhappy situation. And most assuredly, there are situations that do require immediate action.

But that response is not all. For one of the great tasks of humanity at present is to hold only that in one's mind and heart that relate to a higher frequency, realizing that all appearance is illusion, and never the full story.

Your own frequency is your key out of the prison you were forced to build for yourself long ago. That beautiful tone which you sing with your very being is all about freedom from fear, freedom from the stress of uncertainty that many around the world are experiencing.

The beautiful song "Freedom Freedom" expresses this perfectly.[4]

---

[4] The Collective refer to a song on the album "My Oh My It's Time to Fly" by singer/songwriter Rickie Byars. At this writing, the video for "Freedom Freedom" can be found at https://www.youtube.com/watch?v=fJ91GMXLggA.

How far you will have to go is a matter of each individual path. Yet we assure you, you are all of you capable of tapping into those very resources you tucked into your belt before arriving on this planet in this fast-moving era.

None of it is bigger than you are—most especially, not when you stand together.

Find community. Find like-minded Light Bringers who, like you, refuse the petty political arguments of who's right and who's wrong, and who's the savior and who isn't. Those who are not looking to the skies for rescue, but calling on the power of their souls and their higher selves and demanding support, Wisdom, and the courage to face the day.

None of this is beyond you. We see all of you, who wrote the book on facing down tough circumstances in this Universe, and we can only marvel at your refusal to give up. Yet feed yourselves inspiration at every turn, friends! Inspiring music, images, books, films, friends, and your own ability to laugh at the irony and strangeness of the holographic illusion around you—the attempted manipulations, and the purported gains and losses.

Yes! Divine Love is all there is.

And know that in all of this, you are never alone.

9

On Collective Consciousness and Assisting Others on Their Path

How can we, as individuals, help change the collective consciousness in order to effect positive changes in the world?
I feel that until the collective consciousness is aligned, positive change will not happen.

* * * * *

As a Light Being doing my best each day to bring in more Love and Light for myself, what are the best ways I can assist others on their individual paths?

We shall speak to these issues together, as they interweave.
 Know that every form of assistance you bring to others begins with the support you offer yourself. Others look to you, a bright Light in this Universe, for guidance not only via your words, actions, life choices, but mainly by the feeling of your presence and overall energies.
 And so the first step on the journey to changing the world, as we note elsewhere, is not so much engaging in peaceful

demonstrations, emailing government representatives, signing petitions, or stating clearly on what you do or do not support, though certainly these can be positive at times.

For increasingly now, any real life change, and any form of assisting others, always begins within.

Begin with asking yourself how positively you feel about life. Especially during these challenging times of transformation, ask what your overall emotional set point seems to be. These will clue you in to how brightly your Light is shining—how much ease and Joy there seems to be in the Universe, according to your life energies. From there, the question will be how to begin to raise that frequency to where your feelings about life flow at a higher level.

There are many ways to raise your vibration and general feelings about life. Daily practices that assist in this way can be a great help, if they are the right ones for you.

How can you tell? Almost right from the start, the right practice will give you a feeling of relief or Lightness in your heart-space. Then as you continue with it over time, you will gain a feeling of calm or Joy, perhaps inspiration.

We would begin each day in quiet, welcoming the morning with Thanks in your heart. Going into Thanks and Appreciation not only for all you have and all you have come through thus far, but for all the good that is to come. Appreciation for the morning itself. For the Earth Herself. For your own life! Your own body and breath. Your senses. Your chosen time upon the planet. Or all of that, however you wish to phrase it.

After you have gotten dressed and had something healthy to eat or drink, starting with plenty of pure water, you might then go into a space of quiet in which you meditate in whatever way most appeals to you. You might wish to follow a guided meditation, or to go into deep silence, or to visualize.

Or most beautifully, image that you are drawing the Light of the higher realms into every cell and particle of your being.

Then request direction for your day from your higher self. You might ask, "What do I need to know right now?"

This helps you create your day from a place of higher Light and inner balance, rather than simply following the left-brain's

On Collective Consciousness and Assisting Others on Their Path

dictates on what you *must* get done today. Of course you will have responsibilities to fulfill. Yet before you fully begin the day, close your eyes and image the day going beautifully—everything done with more than enough time to spare. Fun moments for you and others, full of humor and connection to Nature, as well as demonstrations of Abundance, Love, encouragement given and received.

You can also offer the tone of "Om," or of any mantra that speaks to you now. Recall that Sanskrit is a language of tonality and pure vibration. The syllables spoken don't simply "mean" one idea or another. They are the vibrational expression of it. "Om"

being the tonal vibration of the All That Is, or the Universe.

So that as you chant, you align with the vibration of the particular reality that that mantra resonates with. This is powerful! Choose a mantra that most suits what you wish to affirm, create, or offer Appreciation for. As you continue to calmly resonate with the vibration of that mantra, its inner Joy, reassurances, and outer fulfillment will flow to you in perfect time and way, as assuredly as you breathe.

After this, we would find a way to stretch the body for a bit—some cannot go without their steady yoga practice. Others prefer a morning walk, or some other exercise that affirms health and movement. This offers the body a chance to meet the start of the day with something positive. In this way, you return to conscious movement. You reassure the body that you will be joined in this day, not moving thoughtlessly through it, issuing unconscious demands and feeling separate from your body, as if it were only a material tool, and not a sacred gift.

You chose to be here in the physical! However you can, honor all your aspects.

Your own life flowing beautifully, smoothly, with Joy and fulfillment, is one of the greatest things you can offer your planet.

If something is troubling you, take time to write out how you are feeling in a journal, or in some other way express what is troubling you. Allow those emotions to come out, rather than denying them until you feel they have dulled sufficiently that they are no longer grabbing your attention.

When that happens, the body and your already very full subconscious must carry the weight of yet another life experience that is unfulfilled, unresolved, and heavy to bear. Worse yet, that sadness, anger, or shock will find ways to express itself in ways you do not like, yet do not immediately connect to the unresolved emotion.

For many, this means an addiction of some kind that masks the unhappiness, or is a distraction from it. That might mean addiction to work, internet, or television. It might mean addiction to drink or drugs or food, or to serial connections that are not solid relationships, and which can leave one feeling even more empty and restless.

For others, it means a life of dulled emotion that blanks out so much that occurs around them, as they prefer to not know the real truth of any one situation—the deeper truth, and the inner result of that in their own and others' lives.

This compulsion to hide and deny one's emotional reality, and true inner needs, is something that has been used to control human beings' thoughts, words, and behaviors for thousands of years. It is a misdirected masculine trait—what some call a "wounded masculinity." It has been pushed upon children of both sexes—"Don't cry! Are you a baby?" A young boy showing emotion is still often accused of "acting like a girl," meant as an insult.

This kind of masculine dominance is then further escalated in the lives of young people. While growing up, and as they go out into the world, they are told that winning, action, and accomplishment are all that matter.

Those cultures that are more heart-based, where emotion is allowed to be expressed, are often mocked by the cultures that are more mind-based. Those in the latter tend to pride themselves on never "letting their emotions get the better of them."

Yet suppressing emotion and ignoring old, unresolved trauma does not create control over them. They will find their way to the surface, one way or another, sometimes in behavior and moments of triggered emotions that anyone would find difficult to process or control.

Many men prefer to be angry, rather than to allow their grief to flow as it naturally must, in order for them to process that feeling. We would challenge men of the current generations to realize how completely this cultural expectation has failed their fathers and grandfathers over many generations. And to see that, in these times of powerful Light flowing onto the Earth, awakening so much in each person, now is the time to allow healing. Even if that means rewriting or ignoring the conventional rules.

We would likewise challenge men to not leave the issue of their own spiritual growth to the women in their life, to take care of for them. This is a tendency we see often, whereas a balanced masculinity will lead a man to want to know his life purpose and the state of his spirit, and how moving further into Light consciousness can assist every part of his life.

We know that as you realize your own wounded inner life, you will move to heal your inner child, your past life selves, your ancestral lineage.

A man on an honest spiritual quest will seek to fully embrace both his masculine and his feminine aspect in mind, emotions, and spirit. He will have come to realize the wounded masculinity of the men who were there (or not there) for him as he was growing up. And he will consciously move to heal that aspect of his spirit and psyche, along with other aspects of his life. This is so for women as well.

You may be thinking, "Healing just myself? Is that the way to assist humanity's consciousness now? Is that the best way to help others?"

And we would say, healing yourself may appear to be outside the realm of helping others. You may feel that logically, encouraging another's spiritual growth, or just listening as they pour out their troubles, is much more important than attending to your own life journey.

"Surely I can do both!" you may think. And we agree. Yet we will say that for your own life to flow beautifully, smoothly, with Joy and fulfillment, is one of the greatest gifts you can offer your planet, and everyone you meet. Your own celebration of life will lead you to fully see and appreciate all around you in ways that cannot occur until you begin to uncover your true self.

That is particularly so now, as the sentient Light particles flowing onto your planet are assisting so many in finally resolving issues they have carried with them, lifetime after lifetime. Certainly you can work with energy healers to heal and resolve the old energy blockages and unresolved reactions to life that you have carried with you for so long.

Yet your own realization that those blockages are there—that they are not you, but a heavy weight you must release now—is again, a great gift to the world.

Because we know you, dear Light Bringers! We know that as you realize your own wounded inner life, you will move to Love and support and heal your inner child, your past life selves, the ancestral lineage that carries that wound as if that were its reality. You will move to release the energy and entity interferences, the mental programming, the old contracts, the many forms of conditioning you have carried for so long.

And in so doing, you will free not only yourself, as you increasingly become your higher self, and fulfill all you planned to create before incarnating. You will also heal your Earth. You will assist with sending into the Light every dark impulse, every dark energy wave and energy transmission installed in Lady Gaia for thousands of years, by a dark network of controllers whose day is done.

You will assist in freeing those who have hurt you, as well as those whom you have hurt, over hundreds of lifetimes on this and other planets.

And you will powerfully assist in freeing whole generations, past and present, of those chains they unconsciously dragged with them through so many Earth lives.

You will have created a vision of a person truly enlightened— living in the Present Moment, in love with Life and its many gifts, shining with the air of freedom, and full of relief over the

On Collective Consciousness and Assisting Others on Their Path

release of all that once squelched your Joy and is now nowhere to be found.

Yes, this liberates a planet! The more that human beings begin to say, "It begins with me, this great Change I have been praying in," the more you take up that sovereignty which cannot be handed you from without, and must be reached from within.

From that beautiful place of calm Wisdom, you will know what else to do, outwardly, to help others.

We are aware that many suffer on the Earth plane now. And we would never discourage you from being kind and supportive toward those around you. Yet your first and most vital mission is to heal or remove all in your own life and energies that dims your Light. All that holds you back from full expression of your most authentic self. All that lies to you, and constricts you into feelings of smallness.

Be of good cheer, dear ones! You ask for a rise in human consciousness, and to be a help to others, and that is a beautiful impulse.

As you shine with that inner brilliance that seeks to radiate outwards, full of the Love you know to be your truest nature, you cannot help but to assist all of humanity, and every living being upon the Earth. In ways so beautiful and so graceful, you astound us.

We are honored to know you.

10

On Galactic Assistance with Healing and Restoring Lady Gaia

In one of your 2021 Message to Lightworkers, it was stated, "There are ways in which the Earth can be protected from the more difficult effects of the solar rays that are reaching you, and ways in which the Earth can be climate-stabilized—ways that have been blocked until now."

Could you please offer what those protective ways are, for both the Earth and humanity, and why they were blocked until now? If they are no longer blocked, what can we expect?

We shall explain that for one, Earth is being assisted by the star families and soul families of those upon the Earth now, as well as by the protective and restorative powers of the higher realms.

Many of you agreed to incarnate at this time (and are often called Volunteers or Starseed) precisely because of the changes occurring now on Earth, in your solar system, and in your galaxy. You and your soul families are here to assist in holding in place a powerful form of protection around the Earth that goes mainly unnoticed and unseen. Yet it does exist.

While not exactly a protective shield, it could be viewed as that, as it mitigates the more intense effects of Sunlight. Not by dulling that Light, but by strengthening the protective atmosphere around the Earth. This prevents Earth from falling into even more extreme weather and climate shifts.

The reason that more complete help has not been more obviously available to you—the reason why Earth's current climate has not been stabilized by your galactic families, for one—is that in order for that to occur, Earth's population would need to be apprised of the galactic presence in an open and conscious way.

Currently, very few people on Earth go through their day conscious of transdimensional star beings as a constant presence, not a sporadic or unproven, "mythical" one. This is so, even though on an unconscious level, nearly every living being on the planet is quietly aware of that presence, deep within. These two forms of experience, the conscious and unconscious, are increasingly meeting now, creating room for more ships to be spotted, for more ships to land, and for more star beings to meet with humans in different places around the world.

Efforts on the part of the old power structure to imbalance Earth's systems are being met with the protection of many millions of galactic missions.

Part of the reason for this, is that humankind has reached a place in its evolvement where the conscious mind allows the eye to see these beings. And yes, for their own safety (from the actions of Earth's military) and for the sake of keeping the population calm and unperturbed, the vast majority of these ships remain cloaked at all times.

Yet if you call upon them, they shall answer.

They will connect with you, if not physically and visibly, then intuitively, and in your dream state. This is for your safety, as your governments currently still monitor physical contact experiences and events.

The protection we spoke of is an etheric one, which Earth and the majority of Her people did not call out for, for millennia, yet which all of you have now called forward. Again—much occurs on a soul level that humankind is not consciously aware of. The current incoming era of the Sat (or Satya) Yuga also calls forward a time of benevolence, of increasing Peace, and of a unity consciousness, evolving toward the consciousness of Oneness and beyond.

So that efforts on the part of the old power structure to imbalance Earth's climate by increasing extreme weather and inducing higher temperatures, are being met with the protection of millions of assisting galactic missions. Within these are the beings who are working with those of you who have come in to be "on the ground" now.

You are anchoring the frequencies of wholeness, balance, equality of all persons, Divine Justice, the honoring and protection of Lady Gaia, and the reintroduction of Earth life into galactic culture. This will not occur all at once, yet it is coming into being. The thing that powerfully speeds it along is the enactment of NESARA law.

With the announcement and enactment of NESARA, the balance of power on planet Earth shifts from that of the old power structure to that of humanity itself. Currently, a few families who are descendants of invaders to Mother Gaia thousands of years ago are still pillaging Earth's natural elements. The greatest hallmark of their usurpation being the downgrading of and control over the consciousness of Her people, which in these upward shifting energies, can no longer stand.

And so there was a blockage regarding how much help Earth could accept in planetary and galactic terms, so long as the Universal era was the Kali Yuga—the era of destruction. That era, now ending, was a time of deconstruction. A breaking down of the old Earth structure, so that the new could be built in its place.

On Earth's current timeline, we see no destruction of Earth life, only the renewal of it.

This is how the Sat Yuga comes into place. The old gives way to the new, due to the cycles of universal movement. As with all else in this Universe, nothing remains the same indefinitely. Earth was either going to be destroyed by weapons of war and mass exploitation, or She was going to outlive the efforts of those who are dedicated to war and chaos.

On a higher level, Earth's survival, complete rebalancing, and healing have already begun.

In part, humanity has chosen Peace, hence the creation of NESARA. And in part, those interdimensional beings around you, who would be powerfully affected by the destruction of a neighboring planet, also decided Earth shall not be destroyed, whether by war or by extreme weather and unlivable surface conditions.

That decision having been made by planetary guardians, Ascended Masters, the Archangels and Angelic legions, and many levels of Light beings, amongst others, it simply remained to find ways to protect the planet energetically, so that even in the midst of an all-out attack on Her natural systems, She would prevail. What we referred to in that Message was a mainly etheric form of protection that surrounds the planet.

There remains, as we speak this, a block to certain forms of galactic and higher dimensional helps. Yet there is still great assistance flowing to Earth and Her people now, at increasingly levels. The remainder of that support, including the complete healing and cleansing of the planet, will be provided once Earth is declared sovereign once more. That is why the full enactment of NESARA law is sought by those in service to the Ashtar Command, whether they are on the Earth or serving in space.

Please be assured that on a higher level, Earth's survival, complete rebalancing, and healing have already begun, including restoration and cleansing of Her waterways, air, soil, and crops. This is already appearing as predominant amongst the potential events on your current timeline.

The era in which you now live has empowered great assistance to come forth now. Yet so have the cries and requests of Earth beings, as you yourselves call forward the changes you desire, including the healing and protection of your precious Mother, who desires only to provide a beautiful and Abundant home for all.

Call upon us, for we are here! As we remind you often, you are never alone.

11

On Raising Children in Tumultuous Times

Approximately, how long will this incredibly challenging time last? Will my 8-year-old daughter live to see the New Earth and a peaceful humanity?

I ask, because all the spiritual sources I follow, including you, are gradually making all of us aware of the hard times ahead (and they get harder every time I read), and how brave we are to be born at this time.

But they seldom mention how long we'll endure this transition.

Are we talking 100 years, or one generation?

We will say that for Earth's people, "When?" is one of your most pressing questions. You have been trained to exist on a third dimensional linear timeline, so that the future feels to hold potential difficulty one moment, and potential fulfillment the next. The Present, your only real point of co-Creative power, is often ignored as you focus on what happened in the past or what might happen next.

This is enough to create a roller coaster effect on anyone's emotions, particularly in this powerful time of transition!

It is indeed challenging to be on the Earth now. Understandably, you desire that all children come to know a planet that is finally at Peace, with all weapons rendered useless, and humanity sovereign and free.

Your information sources do not mention how long humanity must travel the rough road of this transition, because they do not know, exactly. We can see the timeline unfolding, as some of them do as well. Yet it is not our role to tell you "when" or even "how." We do not say that the hard times you see now will only get harder. We always make a point of encouraging Earth beings to actively notice all the good occurring now, in your own lives and in Earth life in general.

All we and others can offer, on this free will planet, is a list of potentials we see unfolding. Clear predictions, especially regarding timing, are unwise at best. For one, the timeline can shift in a split second. And for another, it would never be our role to tell you, "This will happen on or around this particular date." That statement would then build expectation that would actually help to create that event or something similar in human life.

Expectation holds great power. This is why we ask you to employ beautiful and empowering images of what is occurring and what can occur, for your own well-being and higher good, and to do it more often!

We do indeed see the fog you refer to, and understand your impatience to be free of it. Yet can you not see that fog lifting in significant ways, even now?

Decide now to look at the world in terms of, "What new signs are there today, that everything is shifting into greater levels of freedom, and Light consciousness?" This can shift your experience from one of uncertainty and anxiety to one of quiet certainty and calm.

Your negatively slanted news media is one of the first distractions to unplug from, as well as social media.

Be aware that watching news broadcasts and judging the state of the Earth by those dire reports and predictions will undermine your efforts to spot positive change. Many people are addicted to gathering new information in an ongoing way throughout their day, and feel to have lost a support system without those reports ringing in their ear. This is so, even if that information feeds a sense of hopelessness in them that lurks constantly below the surface, and threatens to swallow them some days.

It seems to promise exciting revelation, and that you will be "in the know." Yet too often it only delivers more shadow intent.

You have heard the expression "unplug from all distractions." We would say, your negatively slanted news media is one of the first distractions to unplug from, as well as social media. We understand that many use social media as a way to tell others about their products and services. We would simply caution all those going anywhere near these apps and websites to realize the power of their lure. Stay alert to all shifts in your energies while connected to them.

If you feel your energies lower while on the internet or hearing any kind of news report, it is possible to turn away from them and to reaffirm for yourself, "The Light has won! I AM a free and independent being. I choose my own reality of Peace, Unity, and Abundant Well-Being for all!"

Regarding your daughter, you are understandably concerned for her quality of life. Yet realize (though it may sound cold and unfeeling) that this young one chose to come to Earth at this time, not in spite of the chaos occurring now, but because of it.

She intended this, on a soul level. As with all Light Bringers, she wrote out her life chart with great detail, working on it with great care and high intent. Along the way, she was assisted by those she had chosen as guides, as well as beloved soul family members. (You are one of these.) She then conferred with the Councils of the higher realms, to gain their insights.

Upon receiving approval of her life chart, and having created her network of helps for this Earth life in spirit and in body, at the chosen moment, she incarnated into a fully preplanned arrival, including location, parents, family, culture, and moment on the timeline.

None of it accidental. All of it beautifully intended.

Now, you will naturally point to her young years, in Earth time, and explain that as her mother, you see her as a vulnerable child who ought to enjoy living on a planet that is safe, Peaceful, and Abundant. And we agree with you, wholeheartedly.

Yet look at the evidence of this young one's empowerment! You no doubt sense her resilience, and the ongoing support of not only her Earth family, but also her soul family, which you know is there if you will take a moment in a quiet meditative state, to key into their presence. You are able to speak with her higher self, guides, and Angelic guardians—her Spirit team— and let them know your concerns for her.

Even if you do not inwardly hear the voice of your own Spirit team or your daughter's, you can still receive an energetic download of answers from these presences that will answer your questions, and flow into your conscious thoughts.

Know that the answers are there, and that they will not be withheld from you.

And know that you are able to call in Angelic support and protection for your daughter in all ways. You cannot take away the path she came in to walk. Yet you can call in Divine Protection for her each day that will keep her on that path in ways that are as calm and positive as possible. And you can demonstrate for her each day how that sort of life can be lived.

We do not see your daughter losing her vibrancy, even in these times.

Regarding timing, we can give no clear dates. Yet we can assure you that though much good will unfold over the next 100 years of Earth time, humanity will not need to wait that long for NESARA's unfolding. Earth Herself cannot carry on being exploited and harmed for that long, despite what the powers-that-were would prefer. Even now, that path is being powerfully rerouted, and their plans rendered null and void.

Are we doing all this *for* you? No, dear one. Light Bearers such as yourself and your daughter are rendering this a *fait accompli*. It is simply unfolding in its own time and way.

Consider that the sentient Light particles and solar tonal vibrations coming in to the planet now are lifting all causes and outcomes to a far higher level than would have been possible even a year ago. And that humanity is absorbing that Light at a rate at which your bodies, minds, and spirits can take, without imploding.

As it is, some find the rate at which they are being asked to evolve to be too fast, and too demanding. Many whose souls originated in other planets and star systems find that once in a human body, the stresses of the very broad human emotional range are difficult to balance. This combined with the many ways in which humanity is often manipulated vibrationally, creates a very real internal pressure.

Yet we do not see your daughter losing her vibrancy, even in these times. Looking at her powerful spirit, we see her Earth mission, which she determined was best handled while in a physical body, and see her moving deftly through it. We see her assisting those Light beings who are dismantling the old etheric grid that many call "the matrix," and installing outposts of higher Light vibrations into the Earth.

These ring in perfect vibrational resonance to the natural vibrational grids that stretch across the planet. These are not only raising Earth's and humanity's vibration, but are assisting Earth in healing from thousands of years of abuse.

Were you to work beside her as she travels the Earth in her sleep state, creating new energetic lines of transmission between the ships gathered around the Earth and Earth Herself, you would be overcome with pride at the work your daughter is doing. You would not for anything desire to protect her from full involvement in this crucial hour, which she herself is thrilled to take part in.

Consider the young emergency worker, evacuating people from flood or hurricane or other disaster. They never feel more alive than when doing the work they know they were born to do. Do their parents and other loved ones worry for them? Of course! Yet do they respect and allow their loved one to do what they came here to do?

If they truly love them, they will, yes. And if that emergency worker truly takes their work seriously, no one will be able to deter them from it.

The generations that will see the great change you desire are here now, dear one. Consider that what you see occurring all around you is as definitive and vital as that moment that NESARA's enactment is announced to the world.

Consider that all times are Now, and that the Earth has already returned to the Light. And that the illusion of dark appearance cannot compare to the power and beauty and stillness of time out in Nature, speaking with that Lady whom you and your loved ones came in to assist.

And why would you do such a thing, when it would have been so much easier to remain behind—on the ships or in the higher realms?

You already know, as you know it for your daughter. Neither of you would have missed the excitement of this moment for anything in the Universe.

12

On the Jab and Being at Peace Amongst Divided Views

Why is there so much division over the Covid vaccine, and how can we bring people together?

There's so much hate for people with opposing views. I see people recommending that we withhold medical care and basic necessities from those who don't want to take it.

I see people wishing pain, suffering, and death to those who believe differently from them. I've seen spouses separate over differing views on this. I see people pushing fear from every side, and lies being told from every side.

How can we bring about more acceptance and peace around such a divisive issue?

And how can we remain at peace within, when there has been so much pain and fear in the world the past 18 months or more that, as empaths, can make it so hard to function?

There is great division regarding this topic, dear one, because at the same time that a great campaign of fear and coercion is afoot, humankind is awakening on every level, including its highly intuitive third eye chakra.

So that for many people, all within them that rings with the innate Wisdom of their higher self is coming forward, and beckoning them to listen. To go forward, and to become their higher self.

This has left most people tending to rush to one side of the room or the other on this issue. They feel intuitively that there is an emergency happening, and many feel safer assuming it is only the well-publicized physical emergency they are hearing of. Those more in tune with their inner voice, which calls them to the path of their higher good, also feel as if an alarm is ringing in their ears.

Yet it is not the same alarm as those who prefer to trust the old order of things.

When you see people lining up behind either one idea or the other, they are either realizing they are being lied to by those they were trained to trust and obey, and are therefore objecting to what they are being told to do, or they are feeling they must support the old system. Not because they feel that system to be infallible. Deep down, they know it isn't. But because they see it quickly fading now, despite appearances, and they fear that far greater change.

And so the wide open expanse of individual thought and freedom they feel coming forward now, not only strikes them as strange and frightening. It feels terribly wrong to them, and even illegal somehow. Some have called it dangerous, though on a higher level, they intentionally chose to come in at this time when so much is being revealed. A time when the higher Light is coming in with such powerful intention that increasingly, *only* the Truth can be told on this planet.

This has created the split in paths you are seeing, in terms of conscious awareness of what is happening under the surface. Some will believe that as the surface is sufficiently frightening and unsettling, that that is what must be responded to and placated, at all costs. Others look beneath the surface and realize,

"We are being lied to! This is not so much about emergency, as Emergence."

They see the mobilization of corporations, military, government, and private organizations and individuals being used to push an agenda intended to exterminate the majority of the human race, and to enslave the remainder.

Yet it is failing. And the knowledge of that must hold you in a place of calm now, even when dire reports come in that seem to indicate that the old power structure is winning. Even when those not yet awakened mock the "theories" that say the old authorities are not telling the truth, and are not working in humanity's best interests—that a tiny elite who have held the reins of power and wealth for eons on this planet are doing all they can to maintain their old levels of control.

You have seen how they are failing at this, despite extreme and desperate action on their part. This is part of why they continue pushing various phases of their plan.

The hate that appears to be coming from one part of the population toward the other is not actually hate, so much as fear. They are reacting against "the other group" because they cannot imagine making the choice regarding "the jab" that the other group has made.

Understand that this is a time of division on the planet because of the powerful surge of renewal that is moving into every area of human life. The Light pouring in now has brought the presence of unity consciousness into the room. It may appear to be an ephemeral wish, as so much of the old power structure and third dimensional thought forms are exposed now.

That exposure is showing the depth of the corruption and destruction humanity has lived with for thousands of years. These may appear to be "normal" or "OK" for Earth life. Yet in its increasingly enlightened state, humanity has decided these are *not* OK, and should not be considered "normal."

You are holding, magnifying, and planting higher energies into the Earth, shifting energetic patterns, and creating a higher vibrational reality.

Most of you have etherically traveled to (and many come from) other planets and star systems. You know intuitively that the violence, hyper-control of citizenry, exploitation, and corruption with which Earth has been governed for thousands of years is not how a normal civilization functions. And you know that the planet has been in a kind of quarantine for a very long time, because of the destructive nature of its self-proclaimed rulers, and devolved human consciousness.

In order to move out of this state of ongoing chaos and exclusion from the Galactic Federation, everything on the planet is having to shift. And of course, great shifts are not easy. They can feel like earthquakes or landslides. You may desire for them to be over quickly. All in the higher realms who are actively involved in Earth's and humanity's evolvement are doing what they can to assist the forward flow of progress.

They are working not only to assist in NESARA's enactment, but to help release dark energies and entities from the planet. And to erase the dark energy grid that has surrounded and permeated the planet for millennia to harvest human life force energy.

This issue you are finding so divisive, as painful as it is to witness, is actually breaking up much of the old etheric machinery that formerly, the vast majority had no idea was in place. Now they are beginning to see it, regardless of what side of the issue they favor. It is simply that some see it more consciously than others.

Those who only sense this awakening in humanity and their own heart-mind feel disturbed and unsure about these changes. Those who see it clearly are feeling angry, impatient for justice to be done, and full of desire that all should awaken now.

So we would say, regarding this particular chapter of Earth's Ascension, it is best not to expect things to move more quickly than humanity can integrate. That would result in even more energetic "earthquakes" that would leave much decimated, whether of people's spirits and psyches, or of their social structures. It is a delicate balance, to help humankind integrate the beauty and power of their world's evolvement, and the awakenings occurring now, with how rough and frightening it can seem to leave the familiar behind.

On the Jab and Being at Peace Amongst Divided Views

Many have wondered at times, feeling the changes happening in mind, spirit, and body, if perhaps they were dying. And that is a fitting metaphor, as the old them is indeed fading now, so the new can come forward. Yet that deep-seated fear has been greatly exploited with the spreading of the illness, and the supposedly preventative treatment being disseminated.

Your question regarding how to keep an inner Peace as an empath in very troubled times is an excellent one, and one of the most relevant questions now. For from that place of Peacefulness, you will be able to extend a loving compassion—to yourself, in the midst of great change, and to others, in their time of fearfulness.

You and millions of other Light Bringers have come in at this time not to shame or argue others into change, which was the old paradigm. You have come in at this time to stand as examples of living Light. As Light Warriors, you stand in and protect those places on the Earth where higher Light is pouring through the veins and arteries of higher Light energy grids. You also assist the electromagnetic frequencies that lift the Earth's overall vibration.

That vibration is measured as the Schumann Resonance, which is revealing a far higher frequency now than it has for millennia of Earth time. That is due in part to this being the start of the Sat Yuga—the many thousands of years of Peace and Abundance that will flow to all beings. It is also due to the living elements of consciousness you and millions of others volunteered to offer now, while in a human body.

You are holding, reflecting, magnifying, and planting these higher energies into the Earth Herself, shifting the energetic codes and patterns that Earth life runs on, and literally creating higher vibrational outer forms. All this, despite the actions of very dark intent to eradicate nearly all of humanity and make Earth life nearly uninhabitable.

Yes, you are that miraculous, and yes, you are that brave.

The inner Peace you seek will never come, dear one, from focusing purely on this divisive and apparently threatening time, as the old Earth systems break up, and their true workings and intentions are exposed so as to be dissolved. We would take our mind, eyes, and ears away from the news reports, and step away from arguments and debates.

There will be the temptation to draw others, particularly loved ones, into agreeing with your viewpoint, and even to bring them up to your vibrational level. Yet you are aware that no one can create another's growth and forward movement for them.

Allow all their individual path, and release the need to argue or save others. Whatever they are choosing to experience now, consider that as sacred as the health and well-being they desire deep in their hearts. Have compassion as they reach for what they feel will guarantee their safety. We speak more on this in the next chapter.

Blaze the Transmuting Violet Flame throughout any situation. That Flame is sentient, and will respond to your request, every time.

What you seek can only come from connecting your spirit and conscious mind with a much higher Presence—that of the Universe, your higher self, and if you wish, other beautiful higher beings who desire to be of assistance at this time. We would say that to travel each day without a daily meditation practice now is to be in a rocky state, mentally and emotionally, and in some ways, physically, as sleep and relaxation are crucial now, and do not come easily to one who is stressed and worried about the fate of the world.

That time in the higher realms, or speaking with your Spirit team, or chanting a mantra of Peace and enlightenment—all of that is irreplaceable now, and cannot be relegated to the "When I have time" pile of things to do. It is as crucial as food, sleep, and breathing. That quiet time, and time in Nature, and engaging in whatever inspires you now, will put back what the old order seems to have stolen, as it seeks to diminish the Light.

Guard your energies now, all of them, whether of mind, body, or spirit. And be mindful of when your energies have left you to heal or assist another. Call them back in! Do not leave parts of yourself here and there, amongst your surroundings or around the world. Send Light, when you see another struggling. Send

Light to your Earth governments, your medical industry, your legal industry and court system, your corporations, schools, religious institutions—all of it.

Know that every Ascended Master and Archangel stands with you as you do so, adding their own insight and loving compassion to your efforts. We would say, that to blaze the Transmuting Violet Flame of Saint Germain throughout any situation that is troubling you, and throughout the world itself, is utterly irreplaceable now.

That Flame is sentient, and will respond to your request, every time.

You must break the old rules, old habits, old expectations now, dear ones! Release the need to have it all make sense somehow. It will do so, in time. You desire Unity consciousness, and you desire sovereignty. These are breaking through, and flowing to you. Focus on the beauty of that.

We see that Light growing ever stronger that is your true self, connecting so perfectly with all other Light Beings assisting the Earth at this time.

And we would say, that we have never seen an image of such beauty, power, and poetry, and such ongoing Love for all.

13

On Getting Along with Those Who Choose Differently from You

I am choosing to not get the jab for reasons of maintaining the integrity of my RNA and DNA. I've been hearing for years that our carbon-based DNA is transforming to a Crystalline-based DNA, and want nothing to impair that transformation.

My choice has nothing to do with politics, and I'm taking good measures to maintain excellent health. When I read that it's "the unvaccinated" who are keeping the pandemic going and herd immunity from happening, my heart tightens, even as I sense it not to be true.

Can you offer good ways to communicate with those who believe the unvaccinated are the problem, especially if the whole DNA transformation thing isn't part of their awareness?

On Getting Along with Those Who Choose Differently from You

This is an excellent question, particularly as so many Light Bringers seek to be a support and a Light to others, and do not wish to appear to be simply arguing in favor of one medical or political choice or another.

We wish to say that though you and many have caught on that the jab is part of a dark agenda, and that adverse reactions to it are not being reported by the mainstream media, yet each of these choices is a viable path. It is a matter of expressing one's life purpose and path of growth in different ways.

You are correct that it is important now to speak in positive ways to those who feel that if everyone received the jab, all would be well. We would only say, be aware of any underlying feelings that those who support the jab are on the wrong track in life. That is your view of it, yet for some, it may still be their path, though that may make little sense to you.

It is so that the vast majority of humanity is unaware (or prefers to ignore) that the jab is an RNA modifier that disarms the immune system. And that it contains parasites and nanoparticles and toxins, and in some ways greatly differs from other shots that have been labeled as vaccines.

And it is so that many who happily take the jab without researching either contents or effects have not yet broken free of the programming they have received over many lifetimes to do as they are told, and to never question the prevailing authorities. And so, wishing to be a positive and productive citizen who is not tossed out of their job, ridiculed by family or community, and considered a health menace, they again follow authority.

We will not say what medical treatments (or pre-treatments) any one person ought to get, as that is not our role, and not our intention.

We will only say that medical science is still evolving on your planet to where it is still intentionally connected to high levels of ignorance. You have read of how in former centuries, medical practitioners used bloodletting to bring a patient's fever down, as it was believed they had too much blood in them. And that bathing was generally avoided for centuries, as it was believed to bring on illness.

For those who are unaware of the contents, true design, and intention behind the manufacture of these shots, it seems an utterly viable solution. Most people have done little or no direct research into the contents and effects of the jab. They simply take for granted that what is said in the mainstream media is trustworthy and accurate, and that the rampant censoring of opposing views is done in the interest of public health.

Add to that a wholesale belief in the efficacy and fairness of mandating that thousands of employers require their employees to take the jab—that this will protect humanity on a grand scale—and you have a complete picture of mass compliance to a situation most people have no real information on.

And yet, again—that may be their path at present. You alleviate feelings of conflict or disbelief at their choice by accepting it as their path, whether you understand that choice or not.

The difference between your experience and theirs is not political, but vibrational.

Most assuredly, it can be jarring to be a well-intended, compassionate person, and be accused of "not caring" about the outer effects of one's behavior. To accept an injection or not is a highly personal choice. Yet in this case, people are not only being faced with the threat of job loss and lack of freedom of movement. The jab is also being emotionally tied to family and community welfare.

Heavy propaganda has flowed out from most forms of media to ensure guilt feelings, should anyone wish to abstain, and therefore supposedly endanger all around them. That is coupled with the stigma of being an "anti-" this or that, or a "conspiracy theorist," a clever twist of phrase thought up by your former controllers decades ago.

And yet—were you ever *fully* under another's control? Have not huge swaths of your life always been up to you, regardless of trauma from this or other lives? Regardless of social programming and the many forms of hypnosis in modern life? You have noted the near-constant connections to screens, new

On Getting Along with Those Who Choose Differently from You

information, fast-moving images, and digital games that are meant to substitute for actual skill and adventure.

Yet even amidst all this, you and many millions of others have managed to ask, *What is really happening here? How do I deal with it, and stay true to my path?*

We would simply say, you have the courage required to stay true to your path now. And you have the courage required to allow others their paths, even when those paths seem to you to be pure madness.

So that if you start a conversation with someone who has chosen differently from you regarding the jab, you will not be in that conversation purely with your mind, but with your high heart. Your mind may be full of facts and figures regarding why your choice is the far wiser and healthier one. Though that is your choice, understand that for the person you are speaking to, your path will feel alien, in a different way than theirs feels alien to you.

They may accuse you and others who are avoiding that injection, because that has been the implicit and explicit message they have received for several years now. They trust that they are making the right decision. Patience is needed there, as they base their "rightness" on the supposed inherent "wrongness" of any other decision. And as their thoughts are survival reactions, in their panic, they will indeed accuse others.

Anyone who has made a decision out of fear stands on very shaky ground. That is a very different thing from someone who has taken the time to separate themselves from physical and energetic influences, and asked who is really behind the development of this illness, and how and why it spread so quickly, particularly to nonwhite populations.

And how it is that a shot being pushed upon the population was created and distributed so quickly, when all other such treatments are tested over eight or 10 years' time. Or why it is that the manufacturers themselves state that the jab cannot prevent infection or transmission of the virus. And so on.

Yours is a measured response. Theirs is often (though not always) a knee-jerk reaction. They cannot be compared.

And so, if you were leaving a burning building, and the firefighters had not yet arrived, and others were also seeking a way out of the building, but were terrified, and that terror was keeping them from finding the exit—what would you do?

Would you go into argument with them, while their logical thought was overtaken by a state of panic, and explain how uninformed they were?

You would of course offer compassionate assistance. Yet if some did not believe that you knew a safe way out of the building, and did not want to follow you out, you would have to assist those who were willing to go with you, knowing that you cannot do another's thinking for them.

Before you speak, have compassion for yourself, then have compassion for those who have been manipulated.

We are aware that this choice sounds to be lacking in compassion. Yet we see so many now arguing with friends, loved ones, coworkers, medical staff, and legislators, trying to get them to see what they cannot see, due to their fear or unthinking compliance with mainstream thought. Or in the case of many in government, medicine, and media, because they are profiting from the biomedical industry in some way, or have been threatened into compliance.

Fear is the great thought-scrambler. Once people are afraid, as a senior Nazi officer once commented, you can control them quite easily.

And so the difference between your experience and theirs is not political, but vibrational.

You have trained your thoughts and emotions to remain not only rational, but attuned to the vibrations of the higher realms. And you have been in the habit for some time now of listening to your higher self before making important decisions. So for you, to hear the higher good above the din and clamor of news broadcasts and mass fear agenda is not so great a stretch.

Part of you intuitively foresaw this moment, even from birth. It no more surprises you, on a deep level, than the current climate crisis, and the move toward free energy and breakthrough healing technologies.

On Getting Along with Those Who Choose Differently from You

Yet it is always difficult to see others in the throes of a fear that robs them of their independent reasoning ability, and connection to their own higher wisdom.

So we would say, before you speak, have compassion for yourself, feeling to be the odd one out, and being considered a "threat" to the safety of others, when that is not the case, and would never be your intention. Then have compassion for those who have been manipulated to where they have chosen false claims of safety over the inner wisdom that calls to them at every moment.

That compassion will help you to say little or nothing when others make their accusations or react in shock that you have not had the jab. We would say, the less said, the better, as others are not listening nor responding from a rational viewpoint, but a survival-based panic that blocks out all other possibilities.

Thrown into the mix will be your concern for those who have taken the jab. Know that there are ways to mitigate or nullify its denser effects, though only some of these methods have yet been realized by your natural medicine communities and scientists, and energy workers. Others will come on line, and be known over the ensuing months and years. That is on Earth's timeline.

Great assistance is pouring in from the higher realms.

And do not minimize the power of the ET presence in all of this! For your star families, with the Angelic legions, are working to deactivate the nanoparticles in the serum.

Great assistance is pouring in from the higher realms, within the boundaries set by the law you know as the prime directive, which requires nonintervention in a civilization's development, except under certain forms of extreme destructive action on the part of your former controllers.

This is sensitive ground for Earth beings. And one great reason why this issue is so important to so many at this time! Yet you do not walk that path alone. Nor are we encouraging you to feel it does not matter, for it does.

We would only say, take your own preferences out of the equation, and allow others whatever path they must follow. See them as young souls, only beginning to know who they are.

Those who would trust industries that are looking to maximize their profits through the ill health of others, and a government dedicated to the injection of artificial intelligence into organic beings, are yet small children in many ways.

We do not say this to be condescending or insulting to anyone, including the scientists and doctors who trust these systems. Yet we wish to encourage you to see how much further so many have yet to travel.

And yet—look at the many millions who are abstaining, and proudly so! You are not alone, dear one. We are here, and so are millions of your fellow Light Bringers. Remain calm and centered, and choose to not react from ego-mind or personality when challenged on this or other issues. Let others know you respect their choices and their path, and that you are making the choice that is best for you at this time. Then release the situation, and speak on it no more.

Have compassion for the one whose decisions are based on fear, rather than calm judgment. Walk the path that is highest and best from what you can see and sense at the moment, as you remain open to the direction of your higher self.

Yet respect, Love, and appreciate the utter individuality of each person, and the beauty of that individual path. Surely, you came for this!

This openness, this kind and calm allowing without resistance to the varying outlooks and preferences you see all around you—this too is a great part of your Ascension!

14

On Regaining Higher Dimensional Sight and Awareness

When we have gotten into the fifth dimension, will we see things that are not able to be seen while in the third dimension, like spirits—our [departed] family members, persons from other planets, etc.?

When we are talking with them, will it be more like how it is with folks who have not passed on, where we sit and talk and commune? Or will it continue to be like now? Right now we can talk to them, but not see them.

If we are able to see them, will it be that way with all dimensions, or again, only on certain levels or planes?

An excellent question, and one that is increasingly relevant to Earth life!

For one, you are already able to see things that in the past, you would not have been able to see. The inner, energetic experience (the only thing that is truly real) is something you are already powerfully aware of. You are also increasingly seeing the inner workings of much of your world—that which once hid behind façades of innocence and respectability, that is now being exposed.

This is because the veil that once stood between humanity and the truth of how your Universe works has faded to almost nothing. The actual journey of the human spirit, within and outside of time-space, is finally becoming known.

Increasingly now, your eyes are adjusting more and more to moments such as when someone has entered the room who is not in a physical body. You might visit someone's home or be in a room where you "see" or feel a presence that others seem oblivious to. Your third eye will inform you of a presence that appears perhaps, as an outline of a shape that is barely there. Or you may see someone or something in your mind's eye, and instinctively feel the realness of it.

Your peripheral vision will also increasingly see things physically that your "straight ahead" central vision, run by the left-brain, may not allow you to see.

Though your eyes may more sense a presence than see it as you would an object in the room, you nonetheless know where to look. Your intuitive awareness of energy will also sense a being or energy form near you that in the past might have gone undetected.

Regarding seeing spirits and other etheric beings, it is often the subconscious, as well as the left-brain, that blocks out these images. Most babies are able to see all present in the room, including Angelics, departed family members, the faery realm, the disembodied (discarnates), extraterrestrials, energy forms, and so on. As people grow up and attune to the fear environment human beings have been raised in for thousands of years—also full of left-brain dominance—they increasingly take on the psychic armor and blindfold that effectively blocks their sight of these.

Some never lose the ability to see spirit. Some can also see those beings who do have bodies, but whose molecular density is so fine and high that they tend to go undetected by most people. These can be extraterrestrials, Angels, faery folk, and other beings who are not so easily seen with the left-brain-controlled eyesight, long considered the "sane" or "rational" form of seeing.

For centuries, those who retained their inner sight well, or who taught others how to regain or retain that sight, were mocked, called ungodly, persecuted, or outlawed. Your subconscious remembers those times, in scenes deeply buried in your past life memories. And so in an attempt to protect you from further endangerment, it hides much from you that is actually your birthright.

As with many Light Bringers, you are already beginning to see interdimensional beings by sensing them inwardly.

The closing of humanity's third eye was for the most part an intentional, manufactured process. The current awakening of it is a natural one, as humanity now enters a new era, and calls out to know itself in higher consciousness. On a soul level, you have decided to call back to you those gifts that were long ago buried, either in trauma or due to the discipline, training, and toxic chemicals of the cultures you were raised in.

There are still some cultures for whom these "apparitions" are not "myth" in the sense of a made-up story. Nor are they called someone's "imagination" or a "strange gift." The very immediate and everyday use of higher sight (or sound, or feeling, etc.) found in indigenous cultures is one great reason why the Eurocentric power structure has sought to enslave or erase indigenous cultures for centuries.

As a fifth dimensional being, you will see much that a third dimensional being would be fearful of, or unable to accept as real. Yet it is already a growing part of Earth life. As with many Light Bringers, you are already beginning to see interdimensional beings of varying molecular density by sensing them inwardly, though you may not consider that to be "seeing" outwardly. Yet the sight of the inner eye is becoming increasingly respected and accepted as actual experience.

In truth, all is spirit. All is energetic in nature.

That which is called material substance is simply raw energy gathered into enough density to become what humans call "real" or visible outer form. Yet your inner eyes are increasingly capable of seeing much that in the past would have been relegated to "imagination" or the dream state.

As your ability to discern energy, including the intentions of individual spirits, continues to develop, you will indeed know, via an inner sensing and feeling, when a departed loved one is visiting, whether your physical eyes can see them or not. In any event, you can also speak with them in the etheric by going into a meditation where you locate their essence by calling them to you.

To answer your question—yes, you will sit and speak with loved ones who have passed, once your vibration reaches a level that renders their vibration closer to your own. There are also higher forms of technology that can assist with this. You will not see those of vibrations above the fifth or sixth dimension until you are ready to do so. Yet you can still speak with them in the etheric, requesting their assistance, wisdom, and insights.

As you continue to evolve, and your own density lightens, you will resonate far more easily with fifth dimensional vibrations.

In the higher dimensions, communication is a matter of vibrational transmission. Even names are often offered not as spoken word but as sacred geometry, tonal vibration, colors, and Light forms. Conversation in the left-brain sense of spoken words is not necessary. Gone are the misunderstandings that can come from misuse of language, or differing levels of word meaning. In their place is pure meaning and pure intent, received clearly and accurately.

During channeling sessions, we speak often (both telepathically and aloud) with many people's loved ones who have left the physical. Those persons who are still physically present on the Earth can also be called into the session, in their spirit form. They are able to speak with us about whatever issue the client wishes to speak with them on, because our inner ear is open to hearing them.

Much can be gleaned by speaking telepathically with someone's spirit that they would be unlikely to share in their day-to-day outer form. While speaking from their physical body, a person's personality and ego-mind are more likely to be in control, and can block the high heart from speaking.

Note that whenever you speak with those who have transitioned out of the physical, your instinct will be to speak with them telepathically. Part of you remembers that this is how most speak to one another in the higher realms.

As you continue to evolve, and your own density lightens, you will indeed see much you do not physically see now. Your third eye will continue to awaken to where your physical sight is allowed to perceive what you mainly now experience in your mind's eye, inner ear, or intuitive feelings. Yet those are all utterly legitimate forms of experience.

With the intake of higher Light into the crown chakra, and the awakening of the third eye, all are beginning to have full sight.

One of the reasons that so many are having a challenging time of it on Earth now, is that they are indeed asking to see and know that which is higher dimensional. They are experiencing the steep climb that is Ascension while in a human body.

Relatively few people have attempted this since Earth's fall to the third dimension. Most were taught that the journey of the Ascended Master was for a spiritual leader—a wise guru or miraculous healer—and not for the average person.

Yet both Earth and humanity are reaching well above the frequency you have lived in for millennia, as your galaxy and Universe also move upward in vibration. You are being assisted by astrological alignments and occurrences that signal the start of a new Universal era.

You are aware that there have always been people able to see faery and elven folk, even as adults. There are also many who are able to see the spirits of those who have died physically, but who refused to move into the Light. Or able to see Angelics and other high vibrational beings. It is simply that now, with the intake of higher Light into the crown chakra, and the awakening of the third eye, all are beginning to remember their innate capacity to have full sight.

To recall that ability fully and to put it into use can be a shock to the ego-mind and the survival aspect of the human psyche. Though your ability to see spirit is increasing, yet we would not wait for obvious breakthroughs in physical sight. We would reach out from within, and ask to know now who or what is present.

See if you can discern Angelic presences, loved ones visiting from "the Other Side," or other benevolent beings. Your inner sight is not localized to one spot, unlike your physical eyesight. So open up and let yourself have a look around the property where you sit now, for example. With your inner sight, see if you can spot a presence or two watching over your dwelling and any grounds around it, or wherever you sit as you read this.

Of the two forms of sight, the inner is more important to develop than the outer. All persons now called psychic seers know the power of inner sight, and the ability to discern, feel, and speak with etheric presences, particularly their higher self.

You too are an etheric presence, dear one. And you will indeed speak with increasingly higher vibrational beings, the further you evolve. As you say, you are able to speak with many beings now, whether soul family, departed loved ones, spirit guides, and so on.

Know that the ability to see, sense, feel, or hear inwardly is just as invaluable as the outer abilities. Certainly forms of comfort from your Spirit team, for example, can come to you as you are able to feel their loving presence, as well as to hear or image them inwardly.

Value every part of this journey, whether or not it meets what your third dimensional world calls "actual" seeing and hearing. Your path is too sacred to be judged by the old rules now.

This can be a joyful process. Open up and realize your own forward movement, and celebrate, every step of the way!

15

On Respecting Another's Path and Staying Calm Around Their Energies

Every time I slip into the flow of happiness or 5D, I like to stay in it as long as I can. To feel the joy, and how easy things are when I'm aligned.

Then life pulls me back into 3D, via energies or emotions from my surroundings that I pick up easily—circumstances I (co)created and need to deal with.

I want to live from compassion and loyalty and friendship, but that does usually bring me out of that flow, or at least lowers my vibration. It seems like I can't figure out how to do both.

Does kindness and caring for each other mean we're being pulled into vibrations we need to stay out of? Am I simply confusing things, and should stop trying to save everyone?

As an example, I took the vaccine because I'm a scientist and believe in the skills and good intentions they were created with. I believe in my body's ability to deal with both the virus and the vaccine. Since I'm not worried so much personally about being infected,

I did it as an act of kindness and community, taking care of others.

Lots of spiritual sources advise against it, which seems terribly selfish and misguided to me. Isn't this a collective Lightworkers' trauma/fear we need to overcome?

Can you advise on how to find the fine balance between supporting humanity, but staying out of the crazy energies from the masses?

Regarding your (or anyone's) decision to take the injections, we have spoken of the importance of allowing each person their path, and our answer to your important question on trauma and fear will not vary from that.

As you say, you have made a choice based on your belief that those who created the jab did so using skills and good intentions. As you are a scientist, you will have researched its effects and contents, will be aware of its adverse effects, and know that it is an RNA modifier, and not a vaccine in the traditional sense.

You may also have noted the manufacturers' statements that the jab does not prevent either infection or transmission from one person to another, but is promoted as a way to mitigate symptoms, should one become infected.

And so your taking the jab with the intention that that would help protect others, was entirely altruistic and kind-hearted.

As we are aware of the contents of these injections and the larger intentions behind them, we do not ourselves call any person's objection to taking it misguided, selfish, or fear-based. Again—each must follow their own path.

Many are aware of the adverse events that have followed one or more injections, and are distressed that the mainstream media refuses to report on those numbers. Nor has mainstream for-profit medicine supported reporting these events on the VAERS database. In many cases, medical staff are warned not to report them, even in cases of immediate or near-immediate, post-injection death.

On Respecting Another's Path and Staying Calm Around Their Energies

Many see this, and choose to avoid the jab out of self-protection. And out of refusal to assist the agenda that is pushing the medical community to insist on injections for the masses, despite the immediate or eventual adverse effects, such as a serious illness and a highly suppressed immune system.

Some do feel that their body can deal with the illness and/or the jab sufficiently so as to not feel long-term ill effects from either. To hold that as one's own truth is laudable in many ways. It is so that the mind directs the body, though it does so mainly through the subconscious. And so we would say, for those who have taken it, employ ways in which you can assist the subconscious to ensure that your body will hold up beautifully, and powerfully defend itself from both the illness and the actions of the shots. Natural protocols are coming online now that will assist in this.

Walk the path that is highest and best from what you can see and sense at the moment, and open up to new ideas from your higher self.

It may appear to be a selfish and misguided choice to follow any channel of information, whether this or another, that does not align itself with the prevailing authorities of the day. For a member of the scientific community, it may well appear that the best thing to do in this case is to follow the rulebook for protecting one's health, and to encourage others to do so, according to mainstream medical advice.

We would only point out that this is an era in which people are not only beginning to realize the extent of the influence of the old power structure, and the use of the medical community in exerting increasing levels of control over the populace. It is also a time in which the fear and desperation felt by the old power structure is escalating, as they feel their hold over Earth life fading by the minute. That desperation pushes them to not only create an illness to devastate large portions of the population, but to use it as a means by which to inject nanoparticles, parasites, and toxins into as many people as possible.

Whether you feel that that situation is real or not, it is being seen by millions of people, and those abstaining from the jab have chosen to stand back from what it represents, which is the current transhumanist agenda.

We do not say this to make you or anyone "wrong," dear one. We would say to all, that whatever your decision in this matter, we extend our Love and respect to you and the path you have chosen. That too is sacred, and requires the respect of all who know you.

We would also say to all, that if you feel that someone's decisions are based on fear or lack of information, have compassion for that person, rather than judgment. Walk the path that is highest and best from what you can see and sense at the moment, and be willing to open up to new ideas should your higher self direct you in that way.

As you do so, respect, Love, and appreciate the utter individuality of each person, and the beauty of their individual path, especially when you do not understand the route they are taking at present. Surely, you came for this!

This openness, this kind and calm allowing, without resistance to the varying outlooks and preferences you see all around you—this too is part of your Ascension.

As we speak of in other chapters, being kind and caring does not mean that you must be pulled into lower vibrations. You are not here to save anyone, even loved ones, as that does not empower them. It also drains your life energies, and often lowers your vibration to the level of those you wish to help.

It is part of your path as a Lightworker to learn to remain emotionally neutral as you see others suffering—again, to respect their path, without desire to rewrite it—until you reach the point where you are able to keep your vibration high in those moments. This requires that you be extremely present and conscious of your own emotional state as you see others having a hard time in life.

As an empath, you have spent much of this and other lives feeling others' pain, and desiring to cure them of it. Yet these challenges are why they are here.

As you find yourself reacting to their situation, realize that you are unconsciously trying to take on the energies of their experience so as to save them from it. Yet in those moments, you are also unconsciously trying to heal the same experience within yourself.

And so your path becomes one of noticing those moments when you are triggered emotionally, and realizing that that is your moment to see what you are able to heal within yourself. Be thankful that something has signaled you to be aware of this old trauma, whatever it may be, and seek to heal it.

Some will try various modalities to heal themselves energetically, whether through journaling, Emotional Freedom Technique (Tapping), and various forms of energy clearings and energy healings. Whatever you choose as your help, understand that it is important to allow the triggered emotions to come to the surface and to be fully felt, not denied or plastered over with affirmations. That moment of creating from a higher level will come, but not before you allow yourself to fully feel the pain that has been pulled up to the surface.

Once you have fully felt the depth of those dense emotions, then reclaim your power from them.

From there, you are able to realize that this experience, whether it began in this or another life, or the energy or entity interference, is not truly yours. It is not your true self, and cannot be carried by you any longer. To get to that moment, allow yourself to magnify and fully experience the pain of loss, rage, grief, abandonment, betrayal—whatever it is that has come up to be healed. Allow yourself to cry and work out these emotions in ways that are safe for you (and others). Do not suppress them.

Rather than feel you have failed yourself or your Ascension journey as you feel your vibration dipping down, go fully into that moment, as soon as you can get a moment alone. Ask yourself what is happening—what you feel in that moment. Then allow it to come forward, without censoring, thinking, or evaluating what is happening.

Once you have fully felt the depth of those dense emotions, then reclaim your power from them. Affirm that you are a powerful Creator, and that you created this experience to grow and learn from. Thank yourself for the experience, and the Wisdom and self-knowledge it has brought you. Appreciate the beauty of it, without judgment.

In time you will come to bless and thank these moments as they occur, for they are great gifts! You cannot carry that density with you into fifth dimensional life, and you have no desire to do so. So be glad for those forms of emotional expression that assist you in releasing that which is not yours.

In time you will also grasp that compassion is not a matter of taking on another's life journey, or laboring under what you feel are their misunderstandings, or lack of wisdom. As you allow each person their path, simply continue to shine in your own, as you do what is right for you at this time.

Respect your path fully, and know that it stands separate from all others, no matter how often it intersects with another's, or how fully you are aware of those who feel differently from you on any issue.

As you allow others their choices, you increasingly allow yourself the freedom to live your life joyfully, and not purely in reference to others. All of this is a great part of the journey you are on now.

We see you as you truly are—Light Warriors in an age when the darkness though threatening in appearance is finally being revealed. As with your own dense emotions, it only comes forward now so as to be transmuted into something far higher.

Know that we are with you always. That your path of service and soul growth, and your contribution to Earth life, are utterly invaluable.

And that every moment, you move further into the Light.

We celebrate this with you, and we thank you for welcoming us to your New Earth.

About the Author

Caroline Oceana Ryan is an author, channeler, speaker, and a co-host on *A Night at the Roundtable* on BBSRadio.com.

She has channeled information from Angels and spirit guides since childhood. She currently channels the wisdom and higher energies of the Collective, a group that includes the Ascended Masters, Angels and Archangels, Galactic beings, the Faery elders, the Earth elements, and other higher beings assisting humanity in Ascending to the fifth dimension.

New Earth Challenges is the fourth book in the Fifth Dimensional Life series, which includes *Abundance For All*, *Connections*, and *Earth Life Challenges*. Other popular books channeled from the Collective include *The Ascension Manual – Parts One and Two*. All books are available on Amazon.

In 2014, Caroline published the cultural memoir *Adventures in Belfast: Northern Irish Life After the Peace Agreement*. And in 2020, she published *Lennon Speaks*, a book channeled from the spirit of John Lennon.

She holds an MA in intercultural education and theology from the Union Theological Seminary in New York City. She has published and performed her poetry, and had poetry appear in art installations and art festivals, in the United States, England, and Ireland. Her plays *A Witch's Cross* and *Rage Removers* were produced at the Sunset Gardner Stages in West Hollywood.

Visit www.AscensionTimes.com to sign up for the weekly "Message to Lightworkers" channelings, and for information on channelings sessions, live interviews and events, membership in the Abundance Group, and guided meditations by the Collective.

Other Books Channeled from the Collective

Also from the Fifth Dimensional Life series:

Abundance For All: The Lightworker's Way to Creating Money and True Wealth (2016)

Connections: The Collective Speak on Romance and Friendship (2017)

Earth Life Challenges: The Collective Speak on Dealing with Trauma and Life Changes (2018)

The Ascension Manual series:

The Ascension Manual – Part One: A Lightworker's Guide to Fifth Dimensional Living (2015)

The Ascension Manual – Part Two: Creating a Fifth Dimensional Life (2016)

Also by Caroline Oceana Ryan

Adventures in Belfast: Northern Irish Life After the Peace Agreement (2014)

Lennon Speaks: Messages from the Spirit of John Lennon (2020)

Available on Amazon

Printed in Great Britain
by Amazon